UK MIGRATION: THE ULTIMATE GUIDE TO MOVING TO THE UK

A Complete Guide to Moving to the UK, including understanding UK Visas and Immigration, and Indefinite Leave to Remain.

KEVIN NORONHA

Orders: Please contact your local book seller.

ISBN: 978-1-5272-8323-7

First published 2021.

PREFACE

Congratulations on your decision to move to the UK. The UK is a fantastic place to settle and living here will afford you an enviable lifestyle. There is so much to do and it is conveniently located to the west of Europe, within easy striking distance of the Continent.

I made the decision to move to the UK in 2017. A few weeks before moving, I realised I had left almost everything to the last minute and I knew time was rapidly running out. Part of the reason for this is because the decision to move was almost a last minute snap decision. I thought it would be a walk in the park. But that was before I realised just how much planning, thinking and work is involved with an international move. I had done one overseas move before, but I was much younger then and I had far fewer things to take with me and even fewer matters to take care of before departure.

And so I started doing what I usually do before I go on annual holidays, that is, I started preparing a to-do list and a checklist. Only this one would be the mother-of-all checklists because I would be taking the whole house contents with me, not just a suitcase for a fortnight's holiday in Bali.

Have you ever travelled somewhere, forgotten to pack something critical and then remembered it just as you arrived at the airport? Over the years, this happened to me quite a few times when going somewhere. Isn't it frustrating when you forget to pack something you really need like a charger or one of your favourite garments? Then you end up buying one while you're abroad or at the airport at great expense, which means you end up with two of them when you get back home! So I devised a system for preventing this.

Ideas for what to put on these lists would come to me at random times of the day and night, and in random places (like when I'm in the shower), so I would simply add them to a special spreadsheet as soon as an idea popped into my head.

Moving abroad was similar to this, only the list was much longer as you can imagine. Furthermore, there were many more things to consider – things that needed forethought. For example, what do you do about your bank accounts? Should you notify your electoral office of your intention to move abroad? How about things you're not taking with you – what do you do with them? Then there are club memberships, gym memberships, local subscriptions, insurance policies (car, house, medical) – these will all probably need to be cancelled. There is a seemingly endless list of things to take care of.

In the weeks leading up to my departure, all these lists, plans and notes that I had been writing for my own benefit seemed to grow and soon became cumbersome, especially as they were haphazardly stored in different places – documents on my phone, bookmarks in my browser, information scribbled on post-it notes and stuck in random places. I soon found myself becoming overwhelmed and drowning in information.

The uncertainty of what to do, when to do it and how to prepare simply added to my overall stress. There was almost a feeling of helplessness in that there was no single place I could turn to where I could find all the answers to my questions relating to the big move overseas. Meanwhile, time was relentlessly marching towards my last day.

"Wouldn't it be good if I could have ALL the information I need, consolidated in ONE single place?" is what I thought to myself. "I can't be the only person who's encountered this problem."

So I searched for books on migrating to the UK, and found a few. But they all seemed to fall short. They either didn't have enough detail or they omitted entire topics. For example, what if you had a pet you're reluctant to leave behind? How would you safely and legally transport a pet to the UK? Almost no book I saw talks about how to buy a home, or even what to do when moving into new accommodation. Yet these are all practicalities that need forethought. It was then that I decided to write my own book to address these and other gaps because I was convinced I could do a better job.

There will be a learning curve associated with moving, and one of the goals of this book is to flatten that learning curve and to guide you through everything you need to think about and do, in easy steps, before and after arriving in UK.

It was the English author James Allen who wrote that *Calmness of mind is one of the beautiful jewels of wisdom.* So the other goal of this book is to reduce or eliminate your stress so you can think and plan calmly. With a tranquil mind, you will be more effective and will make better decisions.

How to use this book

Not all of the book will be relevant to you – feel free to skip over sections or chapters that don't apply. I have written this book to be as modular as possible. So just glance at the table of contents, identify which chapters are of interest and then target those. Where you see a case study, this is optional reading but contains potentially useful information. Insider tips are clearly marked. This is information you won't easily find anywhere else either because it's based on my own experience or because it's not common knowledge.

Section 10 contains information to help you plan your move, including a blueprint which is a countdown to moving day, plus a 10-step checklist of critical things to do in your first few days after arriving in the UK.

For your assistance, there's an abundance of URL links throughout the book. I have repeated these URL links, but spelled out in full at the end of each chapter. These are the same as the ones in the body of each chapter. If you're reading the Kindle version of this book, you can safely ignore the links at the end of every chapter. The links at the end of every chapter are there primarily for the benefit of those reading this as a paperback.

With one notable exception, there are no affiliate links at all in this book. You will be given plenty of warning when that affiliate link is coming up.

Welcome to the UK. I wish you a pleasant and enjoyable stay and a successful move too if you have not already arrived.

Best wishes,

Kevin Noronha.

P.S. If you're seeing this on Amazon preview, you can get a free 50-point blueprint to help you in your move to the UK. This will tell you everything you need to do in preparation, and when to do it. To get this, please visit https://easyukmigration.com/blueprint

P.P.S. I have a number of free bonus chapters, including one which is a SECRET bonus. You won't want to miss this. Details of how to get these bonuses are in the book.

Contents

SECTION ONE — THE BASICS & YOUR RIGHTS

CHAPTER 1 — *A Brief Overview of the UK*

Introduction and purpose

This chapter gives a brief overview of the different facets of the United Kingdom (UK), covering geography, politics, its relationship with the rest of the world, and more.

Geography

The United Kingdom (UK or U.K.) is a sovereign state to the north-west of Continental Europe. Once physically joined to mainland Europe by land, it is now separated from Europe by the English Channel under which is a tunnel connecting Folkestone in south-east England with Coquelles, Pas-de-Calais in northern France.

The term "Great Britain" refers collectively to England, Wales and Scotland. Therefore, the "United Kingdom of Great Britain and Northern Ireland", comprises England, Wales, Scotland and Northern Ireland. Respectively, their capitals are London, Cardiff, Edinburgh, and Belfast. The UK is divided into smaller geographic areas known as counties. Counties serve not just for geographic demarcation but also political and even cultural delineation.

There are three small islands which are not actually part of the UK but are still associated with the UK and referred to as “Crown Dependencies”. These are the Channel Islands (comprising Jersey and Guernsey which are both in the English Channel) and the Isle of Man (which is in the Irish Sea). They are largely autonomous and governed independently. The UK has sovereignty over a further 14 territories worldwide but these are not Crown Dependencies, they’re known as British Overseas Territories.

The United Kingdom’s capital and largest city is London, a global city and financial hub with an urban area which houses a population of some 10 million people. Other major cities in the UK include Birmingham (England), Liverpool (England), Leeds (England), Manchester (England), Glasgow (Scotland), Cardiff (Wales) and Belfast (Northern Ireland).

The Queen and her duties and roles

The currently reigning Monarch is Her Majesty Queen Elizabeth II, who was crowned in 1952, making her the world’s longest-serving current head of state. Prior to that, she served her country in World War II during her youth. Today, as Head of State, the Queen must remain politically neutral but she has important ceremonial and formal duties pertaining to the Government of the UK and plays specific roles in the UK parliament based in London, as well as in the devolved assemblies in Wales, Scotland and Northern Ireland. The Queen is the head of the Armed Forces and the head of the Church of England. She is also the Head of State for Canada, Australia and New Zealand.

As Head of State for the UK, Queen Elizabeth represents the nation for the purposes of national identity and cultural affairs. The British Monarchy is known as a constitutional monarchy. That means that although the Sovereign is Head of State, the ability to create and pass legislation is delegated to an elected Parliament. So on a day-to-day basis, it is Parliament that is responsible for running the country (not the Queen). Although the Sovereign no longer has a political or executive role, he or she (whoever it might be) continues to play a vital role in the life of the nation.

Political parties

The UK is a unitary parliamentary democracy where voting is allowed and encouraged but not compulsory. There are dozens of political parties but the two main ones are The Labour Party and the Conservative and Unionist Party (also known as the Tory Party or the Tories).

Government

The United Kingdom is governed by a parliament sitting in Westminster, in central London. Wales, Scotland and Northern Ireland have their own devolved governments whose respective power is delegated from the Parliament of the United Kingdom which is able to enact laws to alter the devolution or even abolish it. Parliament comprises the House of Commons and the House of Lords. These Houses of Parliament are responsible for passing legislation, setting taxes and scrutinising the Government.

Lower levels of government would be local government, which operates at the county and even at the town level.

Health

Through a tripartite structure of primary care, hospitals, and community health care, the National Health Service (NHS) provides comprehensive health care throughout the United Kingdom. Primary care is administered through a system of general practitioners (family doctors), who provide preventive and curative care. GPs often refer patients to hospitals and specialists. Parallel to the NHS is a system of health care operated by the private sector, based on insurance premiums charged to members.

Education

Children generally begin formal education from the age of around 5 and compulsory schooling ends in the year that a child turns 16. This is the minimum legal age for leaving school but many continue on to further education, often in the same institute or school. Education is a somewhat complicated matter and the arrangements vary from one region (country) to another in the UK. Tertiary education (university) usually begins from the age of 18. Again, this is optional.

Currency

The UK uses the Great British Pound (GBP) whose proper symbol is £. Each pound comprises 100 new pence (p). The pound symbol *always* precedes the amount. For example, eighty pounds and twenty pence would be written £80.20 and *not* 80.20£. When using the £ symbol, the pence symbol (p) is not used as you can see in this example. A sum of just 50 pence would be written either 50p or £0.50 but not £0.50p. In some countries, people carelessly use the terms "pound sign" and "hash" interchangeably. In the UK, the term "pound sign" *really* means pound sign (£) and is *not* the same as a hash (#).

National anthem and flags

The national anthem is *God Save the Queen.* This gets changed to *God Save the King* when the monarch is a king. The flag of the UK is the Union Jack. With the exception of Northern Ireland, where only the Union Jack serves as the official flag, the individual countries all have their own flags too.

Flag of the Union Jack

Flag of England

Flag of Scotland

Flag of Wales

Sports

The most prominent sports are association football (soccer), cricket, rugby league, rugby union, athletics, golf, tennis, equestrian sports, motor sports and boxing. Not in any particular order, other sports played are darts, snooker, squash, hockey, netball, Gaelic football, bowls, croquet and water sports.

Holidays

In some countries, a distinction is made between the terms “bank holiday” and “public holiday”. There is no such distinction in the UK. If a holiday is good enough for the financial sector, it’s good enough for the rest of the country! Indeed, the term “public holiday” is rarely, if ever, used. On bank holidays, most businesses including the London Stock Exchange and all government departments are closed for trading.

Climate

Spring is from March to May, Summer runs from June to August, Autumn goes from September to November and Winter is from December to February. It sometimes snows in winter but not everywhere. As a rule of thumb, the rainiest time of the year tends to be between September and February. Some parts of the country are more susceptible to bad weather than others. For example, parts of Scotland and Northern England tend to experience the worst of winter.

There is a long-running joke that it always rains on bank holidays. While there’s some anecdotal evidence to support this view, it is of course not universally true.

Time zone

During winter, the UK follows Greenwich Mean Time (GMT) which is the same as UTC (Universally Coordinated Time). In summer, the UK observes daylight savings (known as British Summer Time or BST). The clocks officially go forward by one hour and this takes place at 2 a.m. on the last Sunday in March. This is government mandated and you cannot oppose it even if you disagree with the idea of daylight savings. So for example, in 2020, the clocks advanced by one hour at 02:00 on Sunday 29 March. This means you would have “lost” an hour of sleep that night. In winter, the clocks revert to GMT and this takes place on the last Sunday in October. For example, in 2020, the clocks went back an hour on Sunday 25 October at 02:00. This means you would have “gained” an hour of sleep that night.

Relationship with the world

The UK is a member of the Commonwealth of Nations, the Council of Europe, the G7, the G20, NATO, the Organisation for Economic Cooperation and Development (OECD), Interpol, the World Trade Organization (WTO) and the World Health Organisation (WHO). It was a leading member state of the European Union (EU) and its predecessor, the European Economic Community (EEC) for 47 years, commencing 1 January, 1973 and ending on 31 January, 2020. It has been a permanent member of the United Nations Security Council since its first session in 1946. The UK is also a member of the Five Eyes intelligence sharing alliance (in partnership with the USA, Canada, Australia and New Zealand), the Nine Eyes and the Fourteen Eyes alliances.

CHAPTER 2 —

A Brief Guide To UK Laws & Customs

Introduction & purpose

This is going to be a brief skim of the surface of everyday basic laws as well as some social customs that you should be aware of in the UK.

The Brits are a friendly and very polite bunch. They're said to be reserved in manners, speech and attire though a sense of humour is almost universal.

On the roads

Always wear a seatbelt when travelling in a car, or a helmet if you're on a moped or motorcycle. It is illegal to break these rules.

Always drive on the left.

You must obey all traffic signs, traffic lights and speed limits – these are all compulsory.

Speed limits are in miles per hour (MPH) and distances are measured in miles and yards.

You must stop at zebra crossings when people are crossing or are about to cross the road – they have the legal right of way.

Show courtesy – allow other motorists to pull into your lane.

Use your horn only in emergency as a warning, not as a rebuke (you will almost never need your horn).

Emergency vehicles (those with flashing blue lights and sirens) always get priority right of way. Do your best to move out of their way.

In shops

There is a "Challenge 25" scheme in operation for buying alcohol. The minimum age for buying is 18, but if a cashier thinks you look under 25, you'll be asked to show photo ID. Just to be clear, the minimum age is 18, not 25.

The minimum age for buying tobacco products is 18 (but that is under review and could soon become 21). Tobacco products are kept behind the cashier in shops, locked in plain cupboards with no pictures on the front of the cupboard.

In public

It's rude to smoke with others around, and it's illegal to do so on public transport, at train stations (even if you're out in the open, on a platform), bus stops and inside public buildings. As such the only place you may do so safely is on a public street or in your own home (if you own your home).

The Brits are famous for queuing up (waiting in line). They take it very seriously and you must never jump the queue. You will get death stares if you do. It's not always obvious where the queue is, so ask if in doubt.

Do not throw litter on the ground in public. Take it home with you or find a public bin (trash can) somewhere.

Do not spit on the ground. This is both disgusting and a health hazard.

Likewise, do not blow your nose directly onto the ground. This is also gross and a health hazard. Use a tissue or handkerchief, then fold it up and put it in your pocket.

Social etiquette

Invitations – never accept an invitation unless you're sure you can go and you intend to go. If your circumstances change and after accepting an invitation you discover you can no longer go, you must notify whoever invited you, and send apologies as soon as possible. If it's an appointment where there will be food catering, you must alert them of any dietary restrictions you have, and you should do this at the time of accepting the invitation. When visiting someone's house, you may or may not need to remove your shoes on entry. It is better to go ahead and do so, unless asked to keep them on. If it's a social invitation, it's best to bring a small gift with you – any one of the following is acceptable: a bottle of wine, box of chocolates or bunch of flowers. A thank-you note or message of appreciation afterwards would be a cool thing to send.

Punctuality – for business or professional appointments, you should arrive at the exact time agreed. For public meetings, plays, concerts, movies, church services, weddings and sporting events, you need to be a few minutes early. For social occasions or receptions, you may arrive at any time within the hours specified.

Meeting strangers – a simple handshake and one of the following greetings: "Hello, how do you do?" or "Hello, pleased to meet you." would be the way to go when meeting someone for the first time. In a post-pandemic world, it would be okay to omit the handshake. DEFINITELY no hugging or kissing, please – this is reserved for friends and relatives.

Eating etiquette

If you have dietary restrictions, you should let your host know several days ahead of time. They'll get alternative dishes prepared for you.

Do not sit down at the table until instructed.

It is polite to wait for your host to start eating, or at least to tell you it's okay to start.

Always say "thank you" when served anything.

Do not reach over someone else's plate to get to something. Ask them to pass it to you.

When eating bread and butter, it's best to transfer a blob of butter on your knife from the serving dish to your plate, and then use that to butter your roll.

Don't bite directly into a bread roll. Break off a piece of your roll first, butter that, then eat it.

It's okay to eat chicken and pizza using your hands – but only at informal social gatherings. Otherwise, stick to a knife and fork.

At formal dinner settings, you might see several sets of cutlery in front of you. Each set of cutlery is meant for one course only. Start with the outermost knife and fork and work your way inwards as each course is served.

Do not slurp soup, and do not eat noisily. These are considered rude.

Never lick your knife or put your knife in your mouth.

Use your serviette (napkin) for wiping the outside of your mouth only, not for blowing your nose.

When the meal is over, place your cutlery on the plate pointing to the 12 o'clock position. This tells others that you've had enough.

Do not use your fingers to dislodge food from your teeth – use a toothpick and cover your mouth with your other hand while you're doing this.

Other dos and don'ts

Do say "Excuse me" if you accidentally bump into someone or come within their personal space – personal space is considered 1 metre (or 3 feet) away.

Do make liberal use of the expressions "Please" and "Thank you". These are very simple but important expressions, and not using them is rude.

Do stand in line (in the queue) when waiting to be served anywhere or in a shop.

Do cover your mouth when you yawn and while you are coughing. Nobody wants to see your tonsils.

Do hold the door open for the next person if they are close by, whether man, woman or child. The exception would be when passing through a security door.

Don't talk loudly in public.

Don't stare at anyone (this is very rude and might cause an aggressive reaction).

Don't belch in public.

Don't ever hock a loogie. I've seen this a lot in other countries (won't mention which ones) but it is completely unacceptable in the UK. In fact, don't spit anything at all. This is just gross and a public health hazard! Plenty of people do, but they are ill-mannered or else ignorant.

Don't greet strangers with a hug or kiss – this is for friends and family only.

Don't pat strangers on the back, in fact no touching of any strangers is a good rule of thumb.

Don't ask strangers personal questions.

Don't ever ask a woman her age.

And finally, while we're on the subject of women…

It IS okay for women to go about their daily activities unaccompanied, including to eat alone without being bothered. It IS okay for women to drink alcohol. It IS okay for women to wear what they want and not be questioned or harassed. People in the UK are very independent and everyone is entitled to the same level of respect regardless of age, gender, creed or ethnic background.

CHAPTER 3 —
Your Criminal Rights

This chapter has a somewhat more sombre tone than other chapters but it's no less important.

You might be tempted to think that as a law-abiding person you never need to think about or concern yourself with your criminal rights. Sadly, plenty of completely innocent people are charged with crimes every year and in the event you are unexpectedly detained or charged, it's important to know what these rights are, regardless of whether or not you're guilty.

In the UK, all persons are equal under the law and as such, everyone has criminal rights. Your criminal rights are vast and extensive and it's beyond the scope of this book to discuss them here. The most definitive and up-to-date source of information to learn more about your criminal rights is the Government page on crime, justice and the law. Here you will find information about your rights if you're arrested, stopped & searched, your rights to defend yourself or your property, your rights under data protection laws, and many more topics. If you are going to spend any length of time in the UK, I suggest you study this site, particularly the sections you think might be most relevant to you. There's no legal mumbo jumbo. Everything you see on the website is written in plain English.

In Scotland, the rules can vary slightly. If you are planning to settle in Scotland, you should also view the Scottish version of the website given above.

Useful sites

Your criminal rights:

https://www.gov.uk/browse/justice/rights

Your criminal rights in Scotland:

https://www.mygov.scot/justice-law/your-rights/

CHAPTER 4 —
Money & Finance

Introduction & purpose

This chapter gives a brief introduction to the money used in the UK and how to open a bank account. It also discusses widely available payment methods and some of your financial rights.

How much does it cost to come to the UK?

You might be wondering how much money to save before coming to the UK. This is a very difficult question to answer and the answer is "It depends". It depends on where you travel from, what mode of transport you use to come to the UK and the ticket you buy, what personal effects you bring and the method you use to transport them, and what visa you apply for. To make things easy, let's make some assumptions:

One person coming alone from New York, on a temporary charity worker visa, not shipping any unaccompanied items. The cheapest airfares I could see on skiplagged for a one-way trip ranged from US$100 to $200. Let's assume US$150. The cost of the visa is £244 (US$316). There is also the immigration health surcharge (IHS) which will be £624 (US$800), which covers one year. If we factor in contingency of 20%, altogether this comes to about US$1500. This would be the absolute bare bones *minimum* amount just to *come* to the UK (not to stay). I should also point out visa costs can exceed £1000, depending on which one you select.

Accommodation and living expenses would be extra. The average Airbnb room is about £137 = US$177 per night although if you stayed for a month, the average nightly price would drop to US$72. For living expenses, there is a brilliant cost of living comparison tool on MyLifeElsewhere. This can be used to compare costs between countries and individual cities.

Notes and coins

The official currency in the UK is the Great British Pound with currency code GBP.

Banknotes issued by the Bank of England are in denominations of £50 (not widely used), £20, £10 and £5. Apart from the £50 note, all notes are made of polymer and the whole range looks very colourful and pretty. To see images of currently-circulating banknotes, please visit the Bank of England's banknote image gallery on Flickr.

> ***Comment***: Notes issued by the Bank of England are accepted throughout the UK, but there is widespread confusion over whether notes issued by banks in Northern Ireland and Scotland are legal tender elsewhere. According to *Which?* consumer authority, they are not legal tender elsewhere and a shop keeper in England or Wales is not obliged to accept a Scottish or Northern Irish note. You can certainly try, but refusal can offend ☺

Coins are in denominations of 50p, 20p, 10p, 5p and 1p. "Penny" is the singular and "pence" refers to the plural. Coins are issued by the Royal Mint, which is a government-owned company.

Banks and building societies

While it is conceivably possible to live without a bank account (many people do), you will face inconvenience and possibly some stigma. As a minimum, it's most likely you'll want to open one basic bank account.

The four main banks (known as the Big Four) are Barclays, Lloyds, HSBC and RBS/Nat West. There are also many others such as Santander Bank and MetroBank. In addition, there are also a number of building societies such as Halifax and Nationwide. When you open a bank account with any financial institution, you will be allocated two reference numbers:

- A *sort code*, which is a six-digit number written in the form XX-XX-XX. An example of this would be 20-79-37. The sort code identifies the bank and the branch.
- A bank *account number*. This is unique to you.

Opening a bank account

Opening a bank account for people who are new to the UK used to be notoriously difficult in the past. Thankfully, things are a bit easier now. You can do this over the phone, online or in a branch. If you choose to do it in a branch, you will need to arrange an appointment beforehand. What are the requirements?

- One form of government-issued photo ID. The most universally accepted document is a passport.
- One proof of address. Different financial institutions have differing policies in regards to the documents they will accept to prove your residence. Among the usually accepted documents for proof of address are:
    - An account statement issued by a bank, building society or credit union within the last three months which has not been printed from your online account. Credit card statements are not always accepted.

- An electricity, gas, water or telephone (not mobile phone) bill issued within the last three months.
- A council tax bill.
- A tenancy agreement (if issued by a local council or registered housing association).
- A mortgage statement.
- Valid driving licence – but only if you didn't use this document to prove your ID.

You might also be asked to quote your National Insurance number when opening your bank account. This is needed for tax purposes. If you don't provide it, you might end up paying higher taxes on any interest earned but if you don't yet have your NI number, don't sweat it because current rates of interest (even on "high" interest accounts) are rock bottom.

How to obtain proof of residence

To satisfy anti-money laundering regulations, you will be required to prove your residential address. But what if you're new to the UK and you can't do that? Here are some options for you to consider:

1. If you're a student, some banks will accept a letter from your university, specifying your residential address.

2. If, before arriving in the UK, you know what your new UK address will be, then you could try asking your bank in your previous country if they will accept a UK address. If they do, have them send you a bank statement to that address.
3. Check if your original bank has a correspondent banking relationship with any of the Big Four banks – Barclays, Lloyds, HSBC or RBS/Nat West. If it does, you might be able to set up your account before you arrive in the UK.
4. Many UK-based banks have international accounts. If you find a UK bank operating in your original country, consider approaching them.
5. Consider hiring an agent to help. A company like 1stcontact, for a nominal fee, will take care of this proof-of-address headache for you. You still need a place where you can receive post, but they have relationships with banks, so they can make an introduction and get an account opened for you providing you have the proof of ID and can prove you have the right to live or work in the UK.
6. There are online financial organisations which can open an account for you which do not ask for proof of address. Examples of these are TransferWise, Monese, Revolut and Monzo.

> You will still need to *provide* an address to receive correspondence, you just won't have to prove it.

Be aware that with options 3 & 4 above there may be unfavourable terms and conditions (such as higher fees, for example).

If in the unlikely event none of the options above works for you, try visiting the Financial Conduct Authority's web page on this subject (https://www.fca.org.uk/consumers/opening-bank-account) for more options.

> ***Insider Tip***: Whenever opening any financial account, always check the terms, conditions and fees. These will outline your obligations as an account holder.

Getting a credit card

Opening a credit card account is trickier than opening a bank account. It helps if you are currently employed. The requirements are the same as for opening a bank account (one proof of ID and one proof of address) and in addition, you would typically need to provide proof of income in the form of bank statements. Some banks (such as Barclays) can give you an indication of how likely your application is to be accepted, before you actually submit it.

> ***Insider Tip***: When applying for a UK credit card, try approaching the institution where you currently bank because you already have a relationship established with them.

If you can't immediately get a credit card on arrival, here are a couple of options for you:

1. **Use your existing card**. Temporarily use your existing credit card(s) from your previous country after moving to the UK. If they're Visa or MasterCard issued, they're universally accepted. But this means you'll pay currency conversion fees as you'll usually be billed in British pounds unless the retailer has other currency options available at the point of sale.
2. **Use a debit card**. When you open a bank account (see above), you usually get an ATM card. This is a debit card meaning it functions as cash but it can generally be used in place of a credit card. This will work if it has either a Visa or MasterCard logo on it.

Mobile payment methods

Apple Pay, Google Android Pay and Samsung Pay are now available. These payment methods have been slow to take off in the UK but their popularity is growing.

Credit history

Opening *most* kinds of financial account, even renting accommodation, will result in the provider carrying out a check of your credit record. They will ask for your consent (although it might be buried in the terms and conditions of the account). Of course, you will not have a credit record when you arrive and any foreign credit history you might have is not considered. When renting your first property, this might mean having to put down a larger deposit than usual (possibly a few months' rent).

Your credit history can be built up over a short time (a few months) by ensuring you pay bills on time, obtaining a credit card and using it to pay for purchases, then paying off your card bill every month in good time. This can easily be taken care of by giving your card provider the authority to direct debit (deduct money from) your bank account when the bill is due. This is the "set and forget" way.

Payment disputes – debit and credit cards

It goes without saying that you should always receive everything you purchase through the post and that it must be fit for purpose. The same is true for anything purchased from any seller, whether in person or remotely. If something goes wrong with the transaction or the delivery, there are avenues for you to pursue in order to obtain redress. The procedure to follow might vary slightly depending on where in the United Kingdom you reside. This explanation assumes you're in England. For other parts of the UK, you should go to the Citizen's Advice website and select your country there.

In the first instance, you should make contact with the vendor and describe the problem clearly. Reputable sellers will make every effort to put things right. If you find your requests are not getting the desired results, you can dispute the transaction with your card provider. For transactions under £100 in value, you need to ask for a chargeback, but you must have approached the seller first, before you approach your card provider. For transactions between £100 and £30 000, you don't need to complain to the seller first. Tell your card issuer you want to make a Section 75 claim.

The chargeback will result in the transaction being temporarily refunded to your credit card account. The vendor then has a certain time window in which to appeal the claim. If they do, and it's successful, the chargeback will be reversed which means you have to pay. Otherwise, if not, it means your refund is permanent.

Comment: I have found that if you're going to become a victim of card fraud, the most likely time of year is in November and December. This is the time of year to be on high alert, frequently checking your card account especially if you buy from sellers you've never used before.

Payment disputes – PayPal

PayPal have their own internal dispute system and you should initiate this within 180 days of the transaction. If this doesn't work and you used a credit or debit card through PayPal, you might still be able to use a chargeback. You need to do this within 120 days of the transaction. If you don't get your money back, there is one further option – you can approach the Financial Ombudsman.

Financial Ombudsman

The Financial Ombudsman Service (FOS) is a service for both businesses and consumers (free to the latter) which helps resolve any kind of financial dispute, even insurance problems. You can think of them as the helper of last resort (that is, when all else has failed). They'll give you their unbiased opinion about your problem and if they feel you've been treated unjustly, they have legal powers they can use on your behalf.

Lessons learned

1) To open a bank account in the UK, you need proof of ID and (usually) proof of address.
2) If you've just arrived in the UK the second requirement will be tricky but there are many ways to circumvent this, in particular, some online banks do not require you to prove your address.
3) Do not close your bank account in your country before your UK bank account is up and running. Likewise, keep your non-UK credit card account open until you have your UK credit card approved.
4) If an online transaction goes awry, there are ways and means of obtaining redress

including disputing the transaction through your card provider. As a last resort, if you're getting nowhere with a retailer, the Financial Ombudsman can arbitrate.

5) Your overseas credit history is not recognised in the UK. A good UK credit history can be quickly built up by paying your credit card bill and other obligations in full on time.

Useful sites

Cost of living comparison tool:

https://www.mylifeelsewhere.com/cost-of-living/compare-countries

How to open a bank account in detail:

https://transferwise.com/gb/blog/how-to-open-a-bank-account-in-uk

Monito – opening a bank account without proof of residential address:

https://www.monito.com/en/wiki/open-bank-account-uk-even-without-proof-residency/

Can Northern Irish & Scottish bank notes be used outside their countries of issue?

https://conversation.which.co.uk/money/reject-banknotes-scottish-irish-legal-tender/

Bank of England bank note gallery:

https://www.flickr.com/photos/bankofengland/albums/72157662787666013

What to do when a purchase goes wrong:

https://www.citizensadvice.org.uk/consumer/somethings-gone-wrong-with-a-purchase/getting-your-money-back-if-you-paid-by-card-or-paypal/

Financial Ombudsman Service:

https://www.financial-ombudsman.org.uk/who-we-are

Help in getting proof of address:

https://www.fca.org.uk/consumers/opening-bank-account

CHAPTER 5 — *SECRET Bonus Chapter*

This entire chapter consists of insider information. It is a bonus chapter in that it's not essential reading. It's a personal story of how I got into a spot of bother with a financial organisation through ignorance, and how it all ended. It contains some valuable lessons for all of us. If you've not already done so, go ahead and pick up your bonus chapters from https://easyukmigration.com/bookbonus

You only have to do this once, and you will get all the bonuses for this book together in one email.

CHAPTER 6 —
Shopping

Introduction and purpose

One of the first things that will occur to you when you set foot in a new country is "Where can I get ___?" Fill in the blank! In terms of knowing where to go to buy stuff, I was like a ship without a compass when I came back to the UK because the retail landscape had changed so much since I had last lived here. But don't sweat it, you will soon get used to things here and learn where to buy what.

This chapter is not intended to be an exhaustive guide to all the shopping options available. In fact, I suggest supporting the smaller, local shops in your area if that is at all possible. I understand that sometimes, they just don't have the range of merchandise you want and it often seems more convenient to look at the bigger shops. In that case, there is a table for you at the end of this chapter that summarises everything. The table doesn't include shops that are limited to certain geographic regions. For example, there is the famous Fortnum & Mason shop which sells premium grocery products. The business is over 300 years old but most of their stores are in London.

Comment: You should drop into Fortnum & Mason if you ever get the chance. Their shops are filled with lots of exquisite goodies! They also do afternoon tea (requires advance booking).

Below I will tell you a bit about some of the most commonly frequented shops plus a few of my own favourites.

Groceries: Supermarkets

Many seem to do their shopping in supermarkets but there are also food markets and farmers' markets. Not all supermarkets carry the same range or at the same prices, and even within individual chains there can be great variation in product range. For instance, Tesco and Sainsbury's have compact mart-like shops in small towns but they can also have superstores away from town centres and cities.

For food and many non-food household items, there is a very big choice of supermarkets and most if not all of them do home deliveries. The big names (in no particular order) are Asda (the British sibling of Walmart USA), Waitrose (part of the John Lewis Group), Morrisons, Tesco, Sainsbury's, Co-op, Marks & Spencer Foodhall, Whole Foods, Lidl, Aldi and Iceland. Iceland, as the name suggests, tend to have mostly frozen food but they do carry some non-frozen foods too.

In supermarkets, there is nobody to bag your goods as you buy them: You will have to do all that yourself. In fact, many supermarkets don't even have single-use bags. They encourage you to buy a reusable shopping bag which is usually very cheap but will last you some time. Most of the larger supermarkets have self-service checkouts.

Supermarket opening hours are varied and usually long. On Sundays, hours are restricted (larger supermarkets are allowed to open for only 6 hours on any Sunday, but they're free to choose their times). Be aware that on major holidays like Christmas Day & Boxing Day, New Year's Day and Easter Sunday supermarkets are legally obliged to close.

Insider Tip: If you find a supermarket you really like and find yourself returning there time after time, see if they have a loyalty scheme and consider joining it.

Groceries: Ethnic foodstuffs

Ethnic foods are very easy to find in capital cities and main centres, and even in smaller towns it is not unusual to see Eastern European or Asian (oriental) grocers, for example.

Convenience stores

Often referred to as newsagents, these shops are widespread and carry essential everyday goods and some groceries. They also sell tobacco products, alcohol, newspapers and sometimes even greeting cards. Their hours tend to be much longer than supermarkets and other shops. They're mostly independently run but a few of them are chains such as Londis, Spar and Tesco Express.

Pharmacies

There are two types of pharmacy. Independent pharmacies and chains. Historically, the independents have given better (or more personalised) medical advice. Contrast this with the typical attitude of a chain store or supermarket, where you're "just another customer."

CASE STUDY: David vs. Goliath in Pharmaceutical Retail

I have a friend whose late wife used to run a pharmacy and a number of years ago he told me a story about how one very large and famous pharmacy chain (you won't find that shop named anywhere in this book, but they're a household name in the UK) wanted to buy out his friend's pharmacy. But his friend didn't want to sell. What did the chain group do? They bullied the owner of this little pharmacy! They threatened to set up a new branch of theirs right next door to him and drive him out of business.

It is for this reason that I started this chapter by suggesting that wherever possible, you should try to support your local shops, especially independent pharmacies. Most of the independents I've seen stock a surprisingly good range of cosmetics and over-the-counter products as well as the usual medicines which need a prescription. The knowledge and usefulness of independent pharmacists is greatly underrated in my opinion. They have as much knowledge as doctors.

There are many medicines (particularly antibiotics) which are restricted, meaning you need a doctor's prescription to get them. These days, no paper prescription sheet is needed. When you go to your doctor, simply nominate the pharmacy where you want to collect your medicine.

If there are no independents in your area (unlikely) or you simply prefer to shop at one of the chains, see my table below for alternatives. The supermarkets also have their own in-store dispensing pharmacies.

Automotive accessories

Halfords is a household name in this space. They have been around for a very long time and stock a vast range of parts. Besides vehicle parts, they also sell bicycles and spare parts for bicycles. Halfords have the largest network of walk-in stores. Call me old fashioned but I still feel that for certain items, it's nice to be able to physically inspect the product before buying it.

Home improvement

Screwfix is my number one choice for DIY bits and pieces, especially tools. They sell a lot of top quality stuff. There is also B&Q which comes in as a close second. In fact, these are sibling companies (both part of the Kingfisher Group) but the interesting thing is that there is not a great deal of overlap between their product ranges.

Other retail stores

There is no shortage of online shops. If you buy on eBay or Amazon, prices can and do fluctuate a lot. You can save an awful lot of money by signing up to a free service like keepa.com or camelcamelcamel.com. On these sites, you can track prices of individual products over time, and set price alerts to be notified when something falls within your price range.

Summary

Below is a summary table of well-known shops and what they carry. Note that Debenhams, a well-respected department store, was just in the process of ceasing trading as this book was going to press. I've chosen to include it anyway, but struck out.

Lessons learned

1) Don't dismiss local independent shops (especially pharmacies). They usually give better and more personalised service.
2) Consider signing up to any loyalty programmes offered by shops you visit often.
3) If shopping on eBay or Amazon (and you're not in a hurry), you can save money by signing up to a price tracking service.

UK Migration

	Groceries	Pharmaceuticals	Health & Beauty	Apparel	Toys	Cleaning Supplies	Home Decor/Supplies	Furniture	Sports Accessories	Appliances & Gadgets	Automotive Supplies	DIY/Workshop Tools	Pet Supplies	Gardening/Outdoor
Aldi	•		•			•							•	•
ao.com										•		•		•
appliancesdirect.co.uk								•		•				
Argos			•	•	•		•		•	•	•	•		•
Asda	•	•	•	•	•	•	•			•				
B&M Stores	•	•	•	•	•	•	•	•	•	•			•	•
B&Q							•	•		•		•		•
costco.co.uk	•		•	•	•	•	•	•	•	•	•	•	•	•
Currys PC World			•		•			•		•				•
~~Debenhams~~			•	•	•		•	•		•			•	
Dunelm					•		•	•		•				•
Euronics										•				
Fenwicks	•		•	•	•		•			•				•
Furniture Village							•	•						
Habitat							•	•						•
Halfords											•	•		
Harveys Furniture							•	•						
Home Bargains	•		•		•	•	•			•			•	•
Homebase							•	•		•		•		•
House of Fraser			•	•			•	•	•				•	•
Iceland	•		•			•							•	
John Lewis			•	•	•		•	•	•	•		•	•	•
Lakeland						•		•		•				
Lidl	•		•			•								
Littlewoods.com			•	•	•		•	•	•	•			•	•

Shopping

	Groceries	Pharmaceuticals	Health & Beauty	Apparel	Toys	Cleaning Supplies	Home Decor/Supplies	Furniture	Sports Accessories	Appliances & Gadgets	Automotive Supplies	DIY/Workshop Tools	Pet Supplies	Gardening/Outdoor
Marks & Spencer	•		•	•	•		•							
Morrisons	•	•	•	•	•	•							•	•
PC World/Currys										•				
Poundland	•		•		•	•							•	•
Robert Dyas						•	•	•	•	•		•		•
Sainsbury's	•	•	•	•	•	•	•						•	
Screwfix										•	•	•		•
Slater Menswear														
Sports Direct				•					•					
Superdrug		•	•											
Tesco	•	•	•	•		•							•	•
The Range			•	•	•	•	•	•		•		•	•	•
TK Maxx			•	•	•									
very.co.uk			•	•	•		•	•	•	•				•
Waitrose	•	•	•			•							•	•
Wickes										•		•		
Wilko	•		•		•	•	•			•		•	•	•

CHAPTER 7 —
Your Consumer Rights

Introduction and purpose

When you purchase anything from any retailer, you are entering into a contract (even without signing anything) and you will have a guaranteed set of implied rights as a consumer. These are known as your statutory rights. This chapter outlines what those rights are.

Statutory Rights

If you ever visit a store you might see a notice about store policy in general, or you might see a remark on your store receipt, accompanied by the words “This does not affect your statutory rights”. What does this mean? This is the store’s way of saying that whatever store policies they have do not change or take away from your minimum legal rights as a consumer. It’s also their way of reminding you that you do have a minimum set of consumer rights to begin with. These are enshrined in law and nothing but government legislation can amend them.

But what are your statutory rights?

The most important statutory rights arise from the Consumer Contracts Regulations and from the Consumer Rights Act 2015. A comprehensive list of your rights as a consumer (including these ones) can be found at this site: https://www.which.co.uk/consumer-rights/regulation. However, don’t be intimidated by all the various acts you see listed here. You'll find everything is written in plain English and there is no legal jargon.

Your most important consumer statutory rights are covered under four pieces of legislation:

1. **Consumer Rights Act 2015** – deals with your rights if the goods you've purchased are not as expected. Anything you purchase must be as described, fit for purpose and be of satisfactory quality. If these conditions are not met, you're entitled to a repair, refund or replacement depending on how long you've had the item. This act extends to services too, including services provided in your home.
2. **Consumer Contracts Regulations 2013** – outlines information a retailer must give you when you deal with them. The information depends on the method of sale, whether online or offline, or by phone. It covers your right to cancel your order, and any time limit on doing so as well as your right to a refund.
3. **Consumer Protection Act 1987** – empowers you to claim compensation against a manufacturer in the event of damage, injury or death. The claims entitlement extends to any affected party, not just the purchaser.

4. **Consumer Credit Act 1974** – in particular, section 75 of this Act can come in really handy. It stipulates that where you've used your credit card to finance or part-finance a purchase with a spend of at least £100 on the card, the issuing bank is just as liable as the retailer. This means, for example, if you never received your goods and the retailer just disappeared, you can have the transaction voided on your credit card and you will be refunded by the bank. This could also be useful if you've purchased a flight, holiday, etc. and the tour operator or airline goes bust after you've paid but before your trip is complete. You will be able to pursue the funds through the card issuing bank. All you need to do is raise a disputed transaction by contacting your bank. You might even be able to do this online, without speaking to a person.

Insider Tip: Although your transaction value needs to be at least £100 to claim under the section 75 legislation, I once found that Barclays Bank was willing to bend the rule and dispute an amount under this threshold, just because they value customer service.

Insider Tip: Any guarantee or warranty will always be in addition to your statutory rights.

Returns and refunds

The rules for returning items differ between buying online and offline. If you buy an item from a bricks and mortar store and change your mind, the shop doesn't have to take it back but many shops do accept returns as a courtesy to the customer, in the interests of goodwill.

On the other hand, if you've purchased something from an online shop, you do have the right to return if you've changed your mind. This is because with an online shop, you have not had the opportunity to physically inspect the product. Instead, you must rely on descriptions and photos. Therefore, there's a higher chance it might be something you're unsatisfied with. You might still have to pay return postage. You have 14 days in which to notify the retailer of your intention to cancel your order. You then have a further 14 days to return the product. Personalised or tailor-made items purchased online may not be returned if you change your mind, unless something is wrong with them.

You will not need to pay return postage for items purchased online which are found to be faulty.

Whether purchasing online or offline, it's worth checking the store policy in regards to returns and refunds. It is not compulsory for a store to have a returns policy but if they do, they must stick to it.

If something you've purchased develops a fault within 6 months and you have it repaired but it's still faulty, you're legally entitled to a refund.

Returns and refunds – exclusions

The Consumer Contracts Regulations has some exclusions for returning goods if the reason for returning them is that you've changed your mind. Excluded goods are as follows:

- × CDs, DVDs or software, if the seal on the wrapping is broken.
- × Goods that have been mixed inseparably with other items after delivery.
- × Goods which came sealed for health protection and hygiene reasons, if the seal on the package has been broken.
- × Tailor-made or personalised merchandise.
- × Perishable products.

Lessons learned

1) You have statutory rights whenever you purchase anything either online or offline. These

rights entitle you to compensation or a refund in the event the product is not up to scratch.

2) Under the Consumer Credit Act of 1974, if an item costs you £100 or more and there is an issue with it, you can also get your credit card provider involved to help you recover payment if needed.
3) Even if you've paid under £100, check with your card provider anyway. They might still be willing to help.

Useful sites

Your consumer rights:

https://www.which.co.uk/consumer-rights/regulation

SECTION TWO — MOVING INTERNATIONALLY

CHAPTER 8 — *How to Transport Your Possessions*

Introduction and purpose

This chapter discusses transporting your personal possessions to the UK. If you're leaving your country for good to come to the UK or if you're vacating your property before coming to the UK, this means you will need to first segregate your items into things you're shipping and things you're leaving behind. This is a golden opportunity to cull your possessions of things you no longer need, want or use. Donate them to charity (thrift) shops or friends/family, or else sell them. If you do sell anything, start the process at least three months ahead of your move, to allow time to find buyers. Don't wait until you're packing for your move, these things will just get in your way and irritate you, not to mention occupying valuable floor space which you'll need for sorting and packing.

Methods of transportation

There are two ways to get your possessions sent into the UK – do it yourself (DIY) or using a removalist service. Depending on where you're coming from and how much stuff you have, DIY might not be an option and is therefore not the focus of this chapter.

> ***Insider Tip***: As a rule of thumb, when you send items by air, you are paying on the basis of weight. When you send things by surface (sea), you are paying for space occupied on a vessel, not weight.

DIY transportation

If you're coming from either Ireland or Europe, one thing you could do is hire a van and drive. You would need to check the hire company's rules on how far afield you're allowed to drive, and where you can drop the vehicle off afterwards. They might also have other restrictions such as age of driver. Hertz, Enterprise and Europcar are companies you could consider hiring from. There are two ferry services available – Stena Line and P&O Ferries. Both allow you to transport your car, which suggests you could take a van instead. They also offer freight services if you decide to send your belongings as cargo instead.

In regards to navigation, vehicle hire companies might try to get you to take a navigation device as an extra. You could simply use a navigation app on your smartphone instead. All you really need is an inexpensive cradle and a USB charging cable that can plug into the accessories socket. Have a paper-based map too as a backup.

If you're coming from further afield, you'll want to send your things using a commercial carrier. The bulk of this chapter is written with this in mind.

Using a removalist

Using a professional removalist is the recommended way of moving, as far as this book is concerned. Using a commercial removalist service will take a lot of the headaches out of your move. First off, if you pick the right company, you will be in good hands and they can advise you and answer all your questions and concerns. After all, this is what they do all day, everyday. A good removalist will give you the choice of packing your own items, and then they do just the transportation, or they can do the packing as well. It will be a little more expensive but it can be worth it just to save your time.

> ***Insider Tip***: If you use a removalist to do your packing as well as the shipping, they will mark your items "PBR" – packed by removalist. The advantage of this is that when HM Customs sees your shipment, they're far more likely to wave it through with no inspection (in other words, they will simply trust the documentation).

Another advantage is that any insurance claim you make for damage is more likely to be honoured if the removalists themselves have packed it. They, after all, are experts who will package all your things both neatly and efficiently, and in such a way that damage in transit is virtually impossible.

Comment: I was blown away with the job my removalist did – ALL of my things arrived in perfect shape after travelling 17,000 km on the high seas.

***CASE STUDY*: Salvage at Sea**

If you are having your possessions sent on water, you need to be aware of the law of salvage. The law of salvage is a principle of maritime law under which any party assisting in the recovery of property at sea is entitled to compensation for doing so. What this means is that in the unfortunate event that the ship transporting your effects runs aground, breaks down, gets stranded at sea, or at worst capsizes, you, along with anyone else sharing the affected container, will be liable for a portion of the recovery costs. This could come as an unpleasant and unwelcome surprise which you probably would not have budgeted for.

The number of shipping containers lost at sea every year could be anywhere between a few hundred and 10,000 depending on who you consult. While some people might freak out at the higher number, let's put this into perspective. The number of containers moved across oceans in 2013 was 120 million according to gcaptain. Even if we took the worst case scenario of 10,000 then as a percentage, 10,000 containers is absolutely minute and arguably negligible. In other words, it is not something worth losing sleep over. Nevertheless, it is something worth bearing in mind.

Fortunately, many shippers offer insurance wherein this particular risk is specifically covered. When taking out shipping insurance, you might want to check that this risk is explicitly covered in your policy. Ask your shipper about it. It may be an optional extra, but considering the statistical risk outlined above, it's unlikely to be an expensive option, so I would advise taking it.

How to screen a removalist

It's likely you'll face no shortage of removalists from whom to select. How do you choose one? Should you go for the cheapest? Not necessarily. You need to remember you're trusting your prized possessions to complete strangers, so you need to feel completely comfortable with them.

Many removalists will give you a free, no-obligation quote. They will reasonably want to visit you at your home to assess how much stuff you have to transport. This is a brilliant opportunity for you to meet a company representative to get a feel for what they're like. You could think of it as a sort of a job interview. I realise that you cannot completely get a full picture for what a company is like on the basis of one meeting with one employee on one day but there are things to look out for.

Do they come across as "salesy"? Are they pushy? Do they put any kind of pressure on you? Hopefully the answer to all of these is "no". On the other hand, do they take the time to answer your questions, ease your concerns and explain everything that's involved and what they can do for you? If the answer to all of these is a "yes", that's a good sign.

Choose a company that takes quality assurance seriously. In regards to accreditation/certification, they should at a very minimum be members of FIDI – the global association of movers. You should specifically seek a company bearing the "FAIM" logo – that's FIDI-Accredited International Removalist. Many a company has gone under in this trade. For companies that are members of FIDI, part of the accreditation component involves proving your financial health. FIDI underwrite the jobs of its members. This means that in the unlikely event your FIDI-accredited removalist declares bankruptcy while your consignment is on the water, FIDI themselves pick up the tab so you don't have to pay removalist fees all over again. And, if you're coming from Australia, make sure they're also members of the Australian Internationals Movers Association (AIMA) – there will be equivalent organisations in other countries.

Questions to ask your removalist

As part of the screening process, here are some questions you might consider asking your removalist. Some of these questions might not be relevant to you, and some of them might be answered on their website. In case you're curious, I have included the answers I was given by my removalist on inspection day. Your removalist might give you similar answers. Wherever you see a question with no answer, it means the question was already answered from their literature.

Filing cabinets and chests of drawers (like a dresser) can be very heavy. Should I empty the drawers prior to packing?

Answer: That's a really great question and the answer is "yes" and "no". For a 2-drawer filing cabinet, emptying is not needed. But a 4-drawer filing cabinet tends to be a little too heavy so we just empty the first and third drawers. For chests of drawers, it depends on the structure and the weight of the item. If it's a good solid piece, and it's only packed with soft items (nothing that can break or spill), leave them as they are. But if it's an Ikea chest of drawers (which tend to be a little bit unsteady when you move them), we recommend emptying them to keep the chest of drawers safe during transit.

For furniture that will be dismantled, how do you prevent the individual components of an item (for example legs of a table, screws etc.), from being separated/lost in transit?

Answer: When we package it (and you'll find this with all the top companies in the industry), we're absolutely meticulous with the inventory of goods we create and a number gets assigned to each and every package/ component. Everything gets ticked off throughout the process. Every time something is moved from one location to another, it gets ticked off again.

Insider Tip: Your removalist will probably maintain what's called a "Priority Box". The priority box contains all screws, nuts and bolts etc. from furniture and anything else that gets dismantled. The idea behind this is that when it gets reassembled at the other end, you don't need to go hunting through umpteen boxes to find the relevant bits and pieces.

> If you're not using a removalist service, you should have your own Priority Box. Use a separate polythene bag for every item and then put all the bits and pieces related to that item in that polythene bag. Then label the bag, seal it, and put it in the Priority Box. Repeat the process for every item needing dismantling.

Should I use a desiccant like silica gel inside my furniture and electrical items? What about putting mothballs in drawers?

Answer: Certainly wouldn't hurt. Both can be found online. Silica gel sachets might even be available in your local hardware shop.

How will you ship long garments like dresses, suits or trench coats—things which are not usually folded?

Answer: We use a flat-pack clothing carton for clothes which is long enough to accommodate long garments. This means no items need folding.

How do you handle paintings, wall pictures, antiques etc.?

Answer: There are a few options. For paintings & wall pictures, we can use a tri-wall art pack with crushed paper inside for cushioning. Alternatively, we can manufacture bespoke high-quality timber cases with gasket seals, slotting, supports and cushioning. Should you require it, we can also manufacture bespoke tri-wall cardboard boxes, cylinders and slat crates.

What sort of security do you have for my possessions while in transit or stored in your warehouse, and are the premises temperature controlled?

What are my insurance options?

Can I track my shipment in real time?

I have a very fragile and expensive musical instrument. How would this be handled?

Answer: I could get a portable wardrobe down to carry it, we could cut it down to size and create what's known in the industry as a "float-pack" and your instrument would be embedded in a sea of crushed paper in the carton. We'd put a "FRAGILE" sticker on the side and we would put it high up on the load with nothing heavy on top of it or around it. It's going to travel nicely that way. If you do decide to send it with us, it will be looked after nicely for you.

What happens at the other end – do you guys unpack, reassemble furniture, and take away the packaging for recycling?

I need time to find a proper home when I get to the UK. Would I be able to have my items temporarily put into storage on arrival in the UK? What would be the arrangements for insurance in this case?

What to leave behind and what to take

The UK has strict biosecurity laws and it's therefore best not to pack any foods in your consignment. Alcohol is another concern because it attracts punitive rates of duty. Wine attracts duty of 40%, and spirits 80% duty. To add insult to injury, you'll be slapped with 20% VAT (sales tax) on top. Give your bottles away to friends and family before you do your packing.

Other items to leave behind (if you're coming from the Americas) are large appliances, kitchen appliances, clothing irons and hair dryers. These items are usually not designed for worldwide voltage and won't work in the UK without a transformer.

Firearms and ammunition should also be left behind, or they'll be confiscated if found in your shipment.

Furniture is very expensive in the UK. So if you have good furniture, consider sending it ahead of you.

UK Customs formalities

If you're going to the UK temporarily, you'll need to fill in form C88. You may or may not have to pay duties on the items you're taking into the UK.

Otherwise, if you're making the UK your primary home, your shipping company will ask you to fill in form Tor01 instead. These forms must be completed and sent to Her Majesty's Revenue and Customs (HMRC). On approving your application, they will give you a unique reference number which you should then give to your shipper/agent. This must be done before your consignment arrives in port.

The ToR (Transfer of Residence) form is just a declaration of facts stating that you're not bringing anything into the country for potential commercial resale, and nothing flammable or combustible etc. Using this form, you will get relief from duties and VAT provided you meet certain conditions. For example, that you've owned for at least 6 months everything you're taking into the UK and you don't intend to sell any item for at least 12 months.

The ToR form does not absolve you from paying duties and taxes on any alcohol or tobacco in your shipment.

Be aware, there could be a backlog of ToR forms for HMRC to process. In my case, the backlog was 8 weeks' worth of forms. As it takes them a few weeks to process the form (that's with no backlog), and give you a unique reference, you need to calculate your deadline for submission of the ToR form based on how long your shipment is expected to take, keeping in mind your application must be approved and HMRC must have issued your unique reference before your shipment arrives in port. Air shipments will take days, while sea shipments will take weeks.

Transporting pets

I have a whole chapter dedicated to this subject (see next chapter). As far as HMRC are concerned, pets form part of your personal property and can therefore be included under a Transfer of Residence application so you won't need to pay duties or tax on them.

Lessons learned

1) Get rid of things you're leaving behind long before you start your packing. Allow at least three months.
2) Seriously consider using a quality removalist – it will make your life a lot smoother.
3) Ask questions – lots of them. The ones I listed are just examples.
4) Insurance is practically a must. A good policy will cover not just your possessions but also salvage at sea (if sending by sea), as well as the cost of transportation itself which alone can run into thousands of dollars.

5) Make sure you get your unique mover's reference number from HM Customs before your shipment arrives in the UK. You can do this by filling in form ToR01 which when approved, provides relief from all duties and taxes (except alcohol and tobacco products).

6) Don't sweat it. If you start early and use a removalist, you'll have few if any worries.

Useful sites

Ferry services into the UK:

https://www.directferries.com/ferries_from_ireland_to_england.htm

Customs form C88 (moving to the UK temporarily):

https://www.gov.uk/government/publications/import-and-export-single-administrative-document-full-8-part-set-c88-1-8

Transfer of Residence (ToR) Customs form (moving permanently):

https://www.gov.uk/government/publications/application-for-transfer-of-residence-tor-relief-tor01

CHAPTER 9 —
How to Transport Your Pet(s)

Introduction and purpose

This chapter discusses transporting your pet to the UK.

The noise, vibration, unfamiliar sights, sounds, smells and people (cargo handlers etc.) are likely to cause your pet considerable stress on the journey. If you're transporting your fur baby by air, there is an added risk in that you have to have faith that the hold is pressurised and temperature controlled (hint: there's no guarantee of either of these things). Some pets do not make it alive or if they do, are distraught when they get to the other end. There was a case of one animal being fried to death in a hold. According to the Washington Post, more than half a million pets were transported by air in 2017 and 24 died (the majority being on United Airlines). As a percentage, this might be a tiny number but it's still 24 too many.

And unfortunately, the UK is one of those countries that require pets to arrive as manifest cargo (as opposed to travelling with their owners in the cabin).

> ***Comment:*** **So I would urge you to seriously consider having your pet re-homed in good time, many weeks (or even months) before you depart for the UK – to allow enough time to find a new home. Let me be blunt here: I suggest you do NOT bring your pet to the UK. I understand that a pet is part of the family but consider putting your pet's welfare first and what the journey might do to your pet. Sure, goodbyes will be difficult and possibly tearful but it might be better for the animal.**

If all of this is not enough to dissuade you from bringing your pet, safely transporting a pet (especially a dog) into the UK while following all applicable guidelines and procedures will be more expensive than your own air travel. Therefore it is likely to be impractical to bring a pet into the UK if your stay in the UK is going to be only a short one.

So you might now wonder why, after that soap box above, this chapter even exists. I know that a certain percentage of readers won't take my advice and will go ahead and transport their pet anyway, and that's their choice. This chapter is for those people.

Before you bring your pet to the UK, make sure you know about and can comply with all the rules and regulations for taking pets *back* to your own country in case you decide to return.

You might be able to get your pet classified as an emotional support animal so they can travel with you onboard in the cabin. This might be something worth looking into. Whether you'll be allowed to do this would depend on the airline's policies and possibly where you're travelling from.

Preliminaries

Check if the company you're using to transport your pet needs documentation to prove your pet is fit and healthy enough to travel.

Only certain travel routes and companies can be used for sending a pet into England, Wales and Scotland. You should check these routes beforehand.

If you're bringing an assistance dog, different rules will apply.

A pet coming from the USA will need a special country-specific health certificate issued by a USDA-certified veterinarian. This certificate will then need to be sent to a USDA office for endorsement. It must be issued within 10 days of travel. Check that the vet used is in fact USDA-certified because using one who isn't, will mean extra expense and time wasted.

Timing of arrival: EU animals

If you're coming from the EU, try to get your pet's arrival date in the UK to coincide as closely as possible with your own arrival. The two dates should ideally be within 5 days of one another. This is known as the EU 5-day Rule. If they're further than 5 days apart, your pet will be considered commercial freight and different rules will apply. Commercial pet moves require a health certificate to be completed and endorsed by a government entity within 48 hours of the pet's departure. If you don't have such a government office nearby, consider getting your pet assessed in a different city.

On arrival into the UK as a commercial move, you will need to pay at least £44 or more, depending on the size of your pet. Add on DEFRA taxes (DEFRA is the agency supervising the laws around bringing pets in to the UK – they can be reached on 01228 403 600 or from outside the UK on +44 1228 403 600).

Your pet relocation coordinator will be able to help with a commercial pet move.

Medical preparation of your pet

This section concerns primarily cats, dogs and ferrets. Pets no longer need to serve that pesky 6-month quarantine period. That requirement was dropped in 2001. Bringing a pet into the UK is now easier and less stressful for both the pet and the owner, at least for cats and dogs. (Rabbits and rodents *do* need to undergo four months of quarantine, if coming from outside the EU).

In terms of bringing property into the UK from abroad, pets should ideally be covered under a Transfer of Residence (ToR) declaration. If you don't have a ToR number handy at the time of your pet's arrival, you will have Customs duties to pay.

The Pet Travel Scheme (known as PETS) is a system that allows cats, dogs and ferrets to enter the UK from EU and non-EU "listed" countries, and has been in place for over 15 years. There are non-EU countries that comply with PETS rules pertaining to EU countries. So this means a pet coming from one of these countries can now enter the UK without undergoing quarantine.

The process is not difficult but you need to get the ball rolling well ahead of your travel date. Allow a minimum of four months. These are the steps you need to follow in this particular order:

1. **Have your pet microchipped** – your vet can do this and it is not painful for the pet. Very important! It must be done prior to administering any vaccinations or other treatments.

2. <u>**Have your pet vaccinated for rabies**</u>. Ideally, your pet should arrive on a one-year vaccine or a three-year vaccine which was administered less than a year before entering the UK. If the vaccine was administered more than a year ago, you'll need to prove that your pet's rabies vaccine never lapsed since the most recent one-year vaccine.

3. **Rabies antibodies blood test** – 30 days after the rabies vaccination is administered, the vet needs to carry out a blood test to check the efficacy of the rabies vaccine that was administered. This test is not required if your pet is coming from the EU or a non-EU listed country.

4. **Observe the 3-week/3-month rule** – if your pet is going to travel under the PETS system, 21 days need to elapse before the pet can enter the UK, assuming your pet is coming from the EU or a listed country outside the EU.

   But if your pet is coming from an unlisted country, you will need to wait three months after the rabies antibodies test described above is carried out. That means, for pets coming from <u>unlisted countries</u>, a minimum of 4 months (that's one month between the rabies vaccination and the associated blood test; plus a further 3 months after that) will elapse before the pet can enter the UK. This assumes the blood test result is satisfactory.

5. **Medical documentation** – when all the waiting periods are over, and you have a satisfactory blood test result for your pet (if a blood test is required), you're then in a position to get the PETS documentation issued by your vet. In the EU, this will be a PETS passport. If it's a non-EU country, your vet needs to prepare and issue an animal health certificate. You will need to sign a declaration stating you will not sell or transfer ownership of the animal.
6. **Tapeworm treatment** – applies to dogs only. Have your dog treated for tapeworm no earlier than 5 days (120 hours) before entering the UK and no later than 24 hours before arrival in the UK. A licensed vet must perform this every time your dog enters the UK, not just the first time it arrives. Failure to do this will result in a 4-month quarantine on arrival. Dogs arriving directly from Ireland, Malta, Finland or Norway don't need tapeworm treatment.

Some anomalies

Pets originating in Jamaica will need to undergo preparation under the PETS requirements in a different country. If you're bringing your cat from Australia, or cats and dogs from the Malaysian Peninsula, there are other special requirements that must be satisfied.

Transportation of your pet

You'll almost certainly need to engage an animal transportation specialist to safely transport your pet to the UK. A good one will be able to advise you of everything you need to know and answer all questions and concerns you might have. You will of course want to make sure your pet is properly cared for while in transit so it is essential to approach multiple companies for advice. Ask them if they'd be willing to put you in touch with past recent clients, just to get independent opinions of the company.

Once you've obtained a transportation plan from a removalist, have a talk with your trusted vet and get their opinion on it. Also ask about any other special medical requirements or advice, recommendations, cautions and warnings. Get a second opinion, if need be.

All this might seem like overkill but remember this is your pet who will be travelling unaccompanied and you need to be certain your fur baby is receiving the best possible care and is transported in the safest and most humane way possible.

Transportation crates for pets

The crate size is crucial. Too small and your pet will suffer stress. Too large and you'll be paying higher transportation fees than you need to. If you have a very large dog, you might need to have a custom crate built. It must be large enough for your pet to stand up and move around.

There are also IATA (International Air Transport Association) regulations that need to be satisfied in regards to the crates that can be used to transport cats and dogs. Among other things, these regulations concern the materials used for the crate, its construction, its size, ventilation, the door, and food and water containers. Other regulations concern the animal's condition. For example, you may not transport a female in season.

Questions to ask your transportation specialist

Here are some possible questions you could ask your pet transportation specialist. Some of these might already be answered on the company's website – so check that out first. Obviously, feel free to ask any other questions you think of yourself:

1. Are your crates compliant with IATA requirements? Are they previously used crates? If so, are they sanitised? At what point do they get sanitised – after the last animal vacates? Or just before my pet will be placed inside?
2. What are the arrangements for monitoring my pet's welfare while in transit?
3. Who will be doing this – will it be medically trained staff or just baggage handlers?
4. What happens in the event my pet is taken sick en route?
5. In light of the ongoing pandemic, how will my pet be kept safe?
6. Do you tranquillise pets?
7. Do you have a detailed list of steps of the entire process, starting from the day my pet is collected to the day it's delivered at the other end?
8. Can you tell me about pet travel insurance?
9. What are my transportation options and their costs?
10. Who holds my pet's passport while my pet is in transit?

11. Can I track my pet's exact location in real time?
12. If so, do you record notes/status updates that I can see in real time?
13. What happens in the event your company or the airline folds while my pet is in transit?
14. What happens to my pet in the event of industrial action that affects the voyage?
15. What accreditations or certifications does your company carry?
16. Can you put me directly in touch with recent clients so I can get some feedback?

Crate training

You need to make sure that the day you put your pet in the crate for travel is not the first time they're entering a crate! In other words, you will need to train your pet to be comfortable with the idea of staying in one of these boxes for extended periods of time. So this is a process that will need to start *many weeks* before the day of departure. PetRelocation have outlined a concise suggested procedure you could follow.

Making your pet comfortable en route

Before the day of departure:

- If travelling by road, get your pet comfortable with road travel by taking short trips around the neighbourhood.
- Obtain a copy of vaccinations and a health certificate, update identification tags and discuss tranquillisation and other precautionary measures.

On the day of departure:

- Make sure the crate is labelled with your pet's name, your name, your new address and contact details, along with special handling instructions. Ensure it also has a big prominent label "Live Animal".
- Place items familiar to your pet inside the crate, such as their favourite toy or blanket. This will help them feel more at home.
- Do not feed your pet a full meal in the 8 hours prior to flying. This can cause an upset stomach (a light meal is okay).
- Ensure your pet drinks plenty of water and is well hydrated. Pack a container of fresh cool water and ensure you stop frequently for walks.

- It's also possible to get certain natural pheromone sprays such as Felliway for cats or Dap for dogs which will help calm your pet. Sprays could also be used in your new home when you get to the UK, to help calm them in the new environment. Check with your vet beforehand if you decide to use one of these sprays.
- Take your pet for a walk or let your pet stretch its legs before they get into the travel crate.

Cost of transportation as manifest cargo

As mentioned above, the UK requires that all pets arrive as manifest cargo. The cost of sending a dog into the UK as manifest cargo will vary depending on where it's coming from and the space occupied en route (dimensional weight). These fees can be upwards of US$1000 for a tiny dog (chihuahua) to $4500 for a Great Dane. These are estimates only and you would of course need to get your own accurate quotes which take into account your own unique circumstances.

Banned dogs

The following breeds of dog may not be brought into the UK:

- Pit Bull terrier
- Japanese Tosa
- Fila Brasileiro (Brazilian Mastiff)
- Dogo Argentino

If your dog so much as resembles any of these breeds, it will be seized and either returned to its port of origin or else put down.

Pet-friendly accommodation

PetTravel.com – these people can help with finding animal-friendly hotels and you can search by city and region, including Northern Ireland.

Going to Scotland? The official tourist organisation for Scotland now has a dog-friendly charter and they rank accommodation in terms of how paw-friendly it is. They have a pet-oriented website which discusses among other things, not just accommodation but other social venues and walking trails for dogs.

TripSavvy have a list of dog-friendly hotels which Wallace the Westie has ranked by giving them a paw rating (instead of a star rating)!

Other useful organisations

As you can see, the process to get your pet moved internationally while not difficult is involved and daunting. Getting something wrong or omitting a step could result in a four-month quarantine in the UK. These companies can hold your hand along the way. They can provide a full service or just advice. I do not necessarily know, like or trust any company listed in this section. This is just to help you get started.

PBS Pet Travel – use international airlines to transport animals under the PETS scheme. They can provide advice and an online quote.

British Airways – provide information for travelling with pets including assistance dogs and emotional support dogs. They operate many of the authorised routes for animals coming into the UK and under the Open Skies scheme, you might be able to transport small pets with you in the cabin.

PetAir UK – an experienced pet transportation company based in the UK. They have an online quote tool and plenty of information.

Find a Vet – an online tool provided by the Royal College of Veterinary Surgeons to help you find a vet.

Other animal transportation companies to consider using: Airpets, PetRelocation, PetTransportEU.

Lessons learned

1) Consider very carefully whether you really want to bring your pet to the UK. It might be better to have them re-homed instead.

2) Always take advice from multiple parties first before transporting your beloved pet anywhere – this means your regular veterinarian and animal transportation specialist companies. Ask questions – lots of them. Better to look silly than leave a question unanswered. You can also contact the Pet Travel Scheme helpline on +44 (0) 370 241 1710. They will be able to give very detailed advice.

3) Think ahead – if you're only going to be in the UK short term, it might not be worth your while bringing your pet with you. Also keep in mind that in the event you subsequently move to continental Europe, the rules for transporting pets to the EU from the UK changed in January 2021.

4) Start the process early. A minimum of 4 months ahead of the move is recommended.

5) Try to time your pet's arrival to be within 5 days of your own arrival in the UK, otherwise it will be treated as a commercial move and different rules apply.

6) Crate training: Get your pet comfortable with the idea of spending long periods of time in the crate. Start this process several weeks before the move.

7) Have your pet categorised as part of your own personal possessions by quoting your Transfer or Residence (ToR) number on the relevant documentation. Doing this avoids having to pay taxes and duties.

Useful sites

Article about animal travel:

https://www.washingtonpost.com/news/dr-gridlock/wp/2018/04/04/more-dogs-die-on-united-than-on-any-other-airline-heres-why/

Approved animal routes into the UK:

https://www.gov.uk/government/publications/pet-travel-approved-air-sea-rail-and-charter-routes-for-the-movement-of-pets

Rules for transporting guide dogs:

https://www.gov.uk/take-pet-abroad/guide-dogs

Transfer of Residence:

https://www.gov.uk/government/publications/application-for-transfer-of-residence-tor-relief-tor01

Listed and unlisted countries from which animals can come:

http://www.gov.uk/take-pet-abroad/listed-and-unlisted-countries

Government information on getting a microchip implanted:

https://www.gov.uk/bring-pet-to-uk/microchip

Government information on rabies vaccination:

https://www.gov.uk/bring-pet-to-uk/rabies-vaccination-boosters-and-blood-tests

Government information on documenting your pet:

https://www.gov.uk/bring-pet-to-uk/pet-passport

Animal health certificates:

https://www.gov.uk/government/publications/pet-travel-certificate-for-movement-of-dogs-cats-and-ferrets-from-third-countries

Government information on tapeworm treatment (for dogs):

https://www.gov.uk/bring-pet-to-uk/tapeworm-treatment-dogs

IATA regulations on pet transportation:

http://www.iata.org/whatwedo/cargo/live-animals/Pages/index.aspx

Getting your pet comfortable with crates:

https://www.petrelocation.com/blog/post/how-to-crate-train-your-dog-for-travel

Pet-friendly accommodation:

https://www.pettravel.com/

https://www.visitscotland.com/holidays-breaks/pet-friendly/

https://www.tripsavvy.com/dog-friendly-hotels-in-the-uk-1661972

Pet transportation options:

https://www.pbspettravel.co.uk/

https://www.britishairways.com/en-gb/information/travel-assistance/travelling-with-pets

https://www.petairuk.com/

https://airpets.com/

https://www.petrelocation.com/

https://pettransporteu.com/

Finding a vet in the UK:

https://findavet.rcvs.org.uk/home/

Declaration that you won't sell or transfer your pet in the UK:

https://www.gov.uk/government/publications/pet-travel-declaration-for-the-non-commercial-movement-of-animals

SECTION THREE — YOUR HEALTH

CHAPTER 10 — *Healthcare*

Introduction and purpose

Healthcare is widely available through the National Health Service. This is a publicly funded service (meaning it's funded through government taxation) and it covers everything from routine GP (general practitioner) visits to major surgery in a hospital. In tandem with the NHS, there is also a private healthcare sector which is subscription-based. In return, you will have shorter waiting times which means you can see specialists sooner and access facilities that are arguably better.

This chapter is concerned primarily with the NHS. If you're interested in learning more about the private system and private health insurance, a very good place to start is *Which?* consumer service.

Medical prerequisites for entering the UK: vaccinations

As such, there are no prerequisites for entering the UK in terms of vaccinations. But it's still a good idea to keep up to date with any ongoing vaccination programme in your own country.

The public healthcare system

Each region of the UK (England, Scotland, Wales and Northern Ireland) has its own NHS body. For the purposes of this chapter, we'll focus on NHS England. For information about the NHS in other regions, visit NHS Wales, NHS Scotland or NHS Northern Ireland.

The Department of Health oversees the NHS in England. A number of third parties (private entities) have been increasingly involved in the day-to-day running of the NHS although the ultimate responsibility is with the Government.

There is no direct charge for hospital treatment provided under the NHS. Remuneration for hospital doctors is salary-based rather than fee-based, though they are allowed to take on private work.

Primary care covers dentistry, pharmaceutical and ophthalmic services. These services do attract charges although concessions apply for patients who are under 16, retired or on low incomes.

What services does the NHS provide?

The NHS provides very comprehensive services as long as you're ordinarily resident in the UK (settled and living in the UK voluntarily and lawfully). Here are some of the services you may access:

- consultations with your GP or nurse;
- treatment in the surgery for minor injuries;
- treatment at accident & emergency (A&E) centres;
- sexual health services;
- maternity services;
- treatment with a specialist when referred by your GP.

You'll still need to pay for prescriptions, dental care and eye care, though there are exemptions for those with serious illnesses e.g. cancer.

Your entitlement to use the NHS

Your ability to access the NHS free of charge depends on your residential status. You need to be "ordinarily resident" or based in the UK. This means you need to be legally in the UK and intend to stay at least temporarily. If you were residing legally in the UK before 2021, you will still be able to use the NHS in England as you did before then.

If you've come from the European Economic Area (EEA) or Switzerland, you can access the NHS with your European Health Insurance Card (EHIC) and you won't have to pay provided your EHIC was issued before 2021 and is unexpired.

If you're from outside the EU/EEA/Switzerland, you will still be able to access the NHS free of charge provided you've settled in the UK and have been granted indefinite leave to remain. Even if you don't have indefinite leave to remain, the UK still has reciprocal healthcare arrangements with a number of other countries. And besides, you can always access emergency services regardless of your immigration status.

Immigration Health Surcharge (IHS)

If you are not able to access the NHS free of charge, you have two options. You can either pay for treatment as you go, or you can pay the Immigration Health Surcharge upfront which costs £624 per year (or £470 for children, students and Youth Mobility scheme migrants). Note that for certain visa classes, paying the IHS is compulsory. When applying for a visa (if you need one), check the conditions for visa approval.

Paying the IHS is not compulsory if you're in the UK on a visitor's visa (but in that case, you'll have to pay as you go for NHS services). There are quite a few other cases when it's not compulsory and it's worth checking if you're exempt from paying. Example include but are not limited to: you're a diplomat, you're a member of visiting armed forces and are not subject to immigration control, or you're in the UK on humanitarian grounds (victim of human trafficking, asylum seeker etc.).

How doctors' surgeries function

Except in emergencies, your first point of contact with the health system is usually your family doctor or general practitioner. To visit a GP, you will usually need an appointment which can be made either by phone or increasingly, online. Waiting times for an appointment can be days or even weeks, depending on your surgery, particularly if your GP is a part-time doctor. Some surgeries consistently offer same-day appointments. You have the legal right to choose your GP.

Appointment slots are supposed to last 8-10 minutes or less but they can overrun especially if your GP has been involved in an emergency earlier that day, which of course will impact all subsequent appointments that day. This means that even if you arrive punctually, you can still be kept waiting.

Your GP can provide general advice and guidance, can prescribe medicines and can also refer you to see specialists. If you require blood tests, there will be a nurse in the clinic for taking blood samples. But you might need an appointment for this. Alternatively, your local hospital will probably have a walk-in pathology unit.

GP clinics usually operate from Monday to Friday and possibly Saturday too. If your surgery is closed, and your problem is urgent, then call 111. If it's an emergency (life-threatening), then call 999 instead.

How to find a GP and register for healthcare

To register with the NHS, you simply select a General Practitioner. You can search for a GP and the NHS also has information to help you choose one.

To register, you need to fill in a GMS1 form and provide proof of ID using a government-issued photo ID document, plus proof of residential address such as a bank statement or utility bill. A surgery will allow you to register only if you reside within their "catchment area" which is a local geographic area around the surgery, and as long as they have capacity. Otherwise, they're not allowed to deny you registration.

Once you've registered, you are then in the NHS system and can access NHS services.

What about non-residents and temporary residents?

If you're visiting the UK and you're from outside the EU, the EEA, Iceland, Switzerland, Norway and Liechtenstein, free access to the public health system is limited. Emergency services and treatment for serious health issues is free. Visitors from the regions and countries mentioned above must have a European Health Insurance Card (EHIC) to get free services. The EHIC covers only unplanned treatment.

If you're a non-resident or visitor to the UK, you will not be able to register at a GP surgery but you can still see a GP during surgery hours if you have health insurance. You're allowed to receive emergency treatment for up to 14 days and beyond that, you will need to register at a practice as a temporary resident for up to 3 months.

What is the cost of medication?

The prescription charge is currently £9.15 per item. It's a fixed price regardless of the medication or the quantity required. Dental charges are given further on in this chapter under dental care. Cosmetic procedures are not covered on the NHS. Low income earners and patients over 60 years of age are entitled to concessions, both for dental work and for medicines.

Eye Care

For a standard eye check, you simply book an appointment with your local optometrist. Expect to pay from £30 to £50. This will cover both a sight test and a check of the overall eye health. Depending on your circumstances, this exam can be free.

Some optometrists (more prevalent in the independent shops) are offering an enhanced eye exam which maps the back of the eye in very fine detail and allows them to detect and monitor changes to eye health. Expect to pay around £75 for this service. If you are entitled to concessions, it will be cheaper.

Dental Care

The NHS provides dental care although many dentists also work privately. Dental care is free for patients under 18 (or under 19 if in full-time education), pregnant women, and women who have given birth in the last 12 months. The following table summarises costs in England.

Treatment tier	Scope of Care	Price
First Band	Routine check, scale & polish.	£22.70
Second Band	Fillings, extractions, root canal work.	£62.10
Third Band	Crowns, bridges, dentures and lab work	£269.30
Emergencies	Pain relief, temporary fillings.	£22.70

In Wales, prices vary from £14.30 to £203; in Scotland, from nothing up to £161.52; in Northern Ireland, from £7.03 to £157.10.

Pharmacies in the UK

Pharmacies are in every town and city. You'll usually see them in town centres or within supermarkets. As I've said in a previous chapter, I feel that independent pharmacies are greatly underrated and I find they provide a more personalised level of care than either the big chains or supermarket pharmacies.

There will usually be a large range of OTC (over-the-counter) medicines but some medicines are not dispensed without a prescription from your GP. You can have your doctor's surgery send the prescription order directly to your nominated pharmacy and be notified as soon as your medication is ready to pick up. In England, you'll usually have to pay a flat charge for your prescription medicine but there is no such charge in Scotland, Wales or Northern Ireland.

Pharmacies are usually open until late in the evening (typically 8 PM or later) and some of them can be 24-hour in main centres. The NHS website can suggest a local pharmacy for you.

If you need to visit a specialist

Occasionally, your doctor might refer you to a specialist. These providers are often based within hospitals. You don't need a referral for accessing sexual health clinics or Accident & Emergency (A&E) departments. When you are referred to a specialist, you can make the appointment online or through the NHS referral system.

In the case of private specialists, once again, you don't usually need a referral but you will be paying the full price for any consultation and treatment.

Other healthcare

Mental healthcare is readily available through the NHS. Assistance and counselling are available for drug & alcohol problems, eating disorders, children's mental health and so on.

Alternative medicine such as acupuncture, reiki and herbal medicine, is available in the UK but access to it through the NHS is limited and the providers must belong to a regulatory body such as the Federation of Holistic Therapists (FHT).

What to do in an emergency: 999 or 112

If you're in any doubt, the NHS has guidelines for emergencies to help you decide what counts as an emergency. Emergency medical care is free in the UK. In an emergency, the number to call is 999 or 112 (both reach the same switchboard). Use either of these numbers when you believe somebody's life is in immediate danger. It is free to call them from any device but you must have an active SIM card installed if you're using a mobile. With no SIM card, your device might still display "Emergency calls only" but this is just the software of your device giving that message.

> ***Insider Tip***: Be prepared for a whole cartload of questions over the phone. If your aural English comprehension is not great, consider getting someone to help you make this call.

Be patient with the operator. The purpose of the questions is to determine the best way to respond to your problem and to prioritise scarce resources. The operator will give you varying instructions depending on how urgent they think your case is. For example, they could tell you to visit your own GP surgery at your earliest convenience and give you instructions on how to self-manage and nurse your condition in the interim. Or they could tell you to make your own way to an Accident & Emergency unit. An ambulance will not necessarily be dispatched for every 999 call.

Comment: If ever you need to check in to an A&E ward in a hospital, be prepared for a long wait (hours). From my experience, you could be waiting for anything up to 12 hours depending on current workload and how the various cases are prioritised.

What to do if you need urgent advice: 111

If the problem is not an emergency, there is another number you should dial: 111. You can use this number if you need to urgently get help and you're not sure what to do. This is particularly useful when your local surgery is closed. Once again, they will interview you over the phone in order to decide the best course of action. There is also an online version for this service at https://111.nhs.uk/

Lessons learned

1) The public health system in the UK is known as the NHS (National Health Service). While it's not perfect, it provides a high standard of very comprehensive care.
2) Access to the NHS is residence-based, not insurance-based.
3) To access the public health system, you must first register with a GP.
4) For certain classes of visa, the Immigration Health Surcharge is compulsory. If it's not compulsory for you and you choose not to pay the IHS, you might have to pay for treatment on the NHS.
5) For emergencies, the number is 112 or 999. Both numbers land in the same place and both carry the same priority.
6) For urgent medical help (not emergencies), dial 111 or visit https://111.nhs.uk/
7) If ever you get admitted to Accident & Emergency, take a book, magazine or game with you (assuming you're well enough to read/ play): It could be a devil of a long wait.

Useful sites

Reciprocal Healthcare Arrangements with other countries:

https://www.nhs.uk/using-the-nhs/healthcare-abroad/healthcare-when-travelling-abroad/travelling-outside-the-european-economic-area-eea/

How to decide when to go attend A&E:

https://www.nhs.uk/using-the-nhs/nhs-services/urgent-and-emergency-care/when-to-go-to-ae/

Registering with a family doctor:

https://www.gov.uk/government/publications/gms1

https://www.nhs.uk/using-the-nhs/nhs-services/gps/how-to-register-with-a-gp-practice/

For urgent medical advice:

https://111.nhs.uk/

Free NHS eye tests & optical vouchers:

https://www.nhs.uk/using-the-nhs/help-with-health-costs/free-nhs-eye-tests-and-optical-vouchers/

Dental charges:

https://www.nhs.uk/using-the-nhs/nhs-services/dentists/understanding-nhs-dental-charges/

Help with dental costs:

https://www.nhs.uk/using-the-nhs/help-with-health-costs/get-help-with-dental-costs/

Help with prescription costs:

https://www.nhs.uk/using-the-nhs/help-with-health-costs/get-help-with-prescription-costs/

The referral system:

http://www.nhs.uk/NHSEngland/appointment-booking/Pages/about-the-referral-system.aspx

CHAPTER 11 — *Finding a Dentist in the UK*

Introduction and purpose

This chapter investigates dental services and their expected costs – both on the NHS and privately.

Public vs. private dental care

If you're new to the UK, there are no issues in regards to accessing the dental system. As long as you are already registered on the NHS, it means you can access dental services through the NHS. Be aware that for any NHS dental services you do access, there could be a lengthy waiting period. Resources in the public dental health system are stretched. Many opt for private health insurance. The perceived advantages are better access to dental care, a better standard of care, and of course shorter waiting times.

What to expect from a dentist

All dental health professionals in the UK need to be registered with the General Dental Council (GDC). This body sets out standards of practice expected of practitioners working in the industry. Particularly noteworthy is that they must put patients' interests first and have a clear and effective complaints procedure in place.

Dealing with dental emergencies

If you have an urgent dental issue and your dentist is closed, you have a number of options:

1. Call your dentist even if they're closed. On their answering message, they might include information regarding how to get out-of-hours services.
2. Alternatively, call the NHS urgent enquiries line on 111. You could also visit 111.nhs.uk. These services are available 24/7.
3. If you have a swollen face, are bleeding or have suffered trauma, or painkillers are not working, visit the Accident & Emergency (A&E) department of your nearest hospital.

What does it cost to see a dentist?

Of course, this depends on a number of things. Firstly, whether you choose the private route or see a dentist through the NHS (most dentists provide NHS services and private services in tandem). It also depends on what treatment you receive and, should you choose to see a dentist privately, it depends on the dentist you use.

The best, most complete and most up-to-date source of data concerning pricing for various treatments can be found on the *Which?* consumer dental costs web page. If you live in Wales, Scotland or Northern Ireland, there are also links to dental costs in those regions.

Concessions

For certain groups of people, seeing a dentist is free on the NHS. Examples of these are:

- Patients under 18 years of age or full-time students under 19 years of age.
- Pregnant patients and those who have given birth within the last 12 months.
- Those receiving income support.

Should you take out a dental insurance policy?

If you're planning to get treatment privately, it's worth considering whether it's worthwhile taking out an insurance policy. The annual cost of policies can range from £126 up to £399 (source: *Which?*). If you're going to be taking out a general health insurance policy, you should check whether that policy includes (or can include) dental work and what the limits and conditions are.

When taking out dental health cover, it's important to remember there are limits not just on the amounts you can claim for the various types of treatment but also on how long you need to hold your policy before you're eligible to make a claim. There could also be annual limits on the number of times you can claim for a particular type of treatment. These factors all need to be weighed up.

If you consider yourself young and healthy, you might choose to skip the general health insurance policy and opt just for a dental-only policy. There is a comparison table of various dental insurance policies on the *Which?* dental insurance policy comparison page.

Lessons learned

1) You can see a dentist either through the NHS or privately. If you see a dentist privately, you will have more choice and control but you will have to pay premiums and there may be claims limits. Seeing a dentist on the NHS might entail many days and weeks of waiting.
2) Find out your local dentist's out-of-hours contact details and store them safely somewhere. For urgent care after hours, ring the surgery anyway to see if these details are on their answering message. You could also try the NHS hotline

111. In an emergency, go to the Accident & Emergency unit at your local hospital or ring 999.

3) Seeing a dentist on the NHS is not free. However, it is cheaper than seeing a dentist privately. All of the following patients may see NHS dentists for free: Patients under 18 (or 19 if in full time education), pregnant women, those on income support.

Useful sites

Expected standards of care of dentistry:

http://standards.gdc-uk.org/

Costs of dental treatment:

https://www.which.co.uk/reviews/dentists/article/private-and-nhs-dental-charges

Private dental insurance comparison:

https://www.which.co.uk/money/insurance/dental-insurance/dental-insurance-explained-ars1c3n889c4

CHAPTER 12 —
Hospitals and the EHIC

Introduction and purpose

This chapter gives a quick introduction to hospitals in the UK including how they work from the point of view of the patient, and also discusses the European Health Insurance Card (EHIC).

Types of hospital

There are two types of hospital in the UK – private and public. You have to pay directly to use a private hospital but public hospitals fall under the NHS. Some hospitals are dedicated to one thing, for example eye hospitals. The quality and service is generally good in UK hospitals. University hospitals tend to have more cutting-edge facilities.

Visiting a hospital

Most general hospitals have an Accident and Emergency (A&E) department as well as surgery, aged care, maternity services and outpatient services. As a patient, you would be admitted to hospital only by way of referral from your doctor or in case of emergency. You will be either an outpatient (going in for a procedure or inspection which does not require an overnight stay) or as an inpatient (which means spending at least one night there).

You will need to make an appointment; though sometimes, if your doctor refers you as an outpatient, the health authority will make an appointment for you and then send you a letter to advise you of the date, time and venue and any other relevant information or instructions. Be aware that if you change or cancel your NHS hospital appointment more than once, your referral will be thrown out and you will need to go back to your GP to get another referral.

You will usually be allowed to choose the hospital you'd like to attend as well as the specialist. You can also request to be treated in a private hospital but you will pay.

When receiving treatment at a hospital, it's not uncommon to have to sign a consent form. This is to make sure that everyone is on the same page about what is going to happen during your appointment.

Your entitlement to hospital treatment

If you need hospital treatment, you're entitled to receive it whether you're a temporary or permanent resident of the UK. You're entitled to free emergency treatment and maternity care even if you're a temporary resident.

European Health Insurance Card (EHIC)

Prior to Brexit, the EHIC allowed citizens of the EU/EEA as well as those from Norway, Iceland, Switzerland and Liechtenstein to access medical services in the UK. Anyone holding an EHIC may use that document to access medical services in any participating country for free or at greatly reduced rates. It means you can take your EHIC and receive urgent treatment from any doctor or hospital in the EU (non-urgent treatment is not covered). Prior to Brexit, the UK was part of this agreement.

After Brexit: Is your EHIC still valid?

According to the BBC, a deal was announced in December 2020 concerning health cards. The article says that EHIC cards which were issued before the end of 2020 will continue to be valid until their expiry date (whenever that is). Going forward, you'll be able to apply for a Global Health Insurance Card (GHIC) which will be the UK equivalent of the EHIC.

Government advice says that if you've come from Switzerland, Liechtenstein or Iceland to the UK on a temporary visit and you arrived before 2021, you'll be able to access "medically necessary" treatment as long as your visit lasts. Otherwise, if you're from one of these countries and you arrive after 2020, you will need to buy health insurance before arriving. Alternatively, you could simply pay for NHS treatment at the full rate, but there will also be a 50% surcharge on top of that.

Healthcare for non-EU citizens

What if you're from outside the EU? The UK still has reciprocal healthcare arrangements with a number of non-EU countries including Australia and New Zealand. Under these arrangements, certain treatments are available at concessionary rates and in some cases, is free. Follow the link for more details.

How to use a EHIC

Carry your EHIC when travelling to the UK or EU country. Present it to staff when receiving medical treatment. In some cases, you can use this card with private doctors but you should clarify this with the doctor as well as with the authority that issued your card.

Most of the time treatment will be free. You might have to pay at the time of treatment and then claim the costs back later, or in some cases no money needs to change hands at all, if state healthcare happens to be free in the country you're visiting.

EHIC: Scope of coverage

Your EHIC covers you for urgent, unexpected treatment; for example, if you break an arm or you catch a disease/virus while you're travelling. As well as this, it also covers you for any ongoing routine care you usually have in your own country as a result of pre-existing medical conditions. It does not cover childbirth, except if a patient goes into unexpectedly early labour. It is forbidden to travel to a specific country with an EHIC with the intention of giving birth in that country. However, prenatal care is covered.

Check that the hospital where you're receiving any treatment is a public one. If it's a private one, you might not be covered under your EHIC.

EHIC: Applying and renewing

The card is usually valid for five years and is issued by your home country or original country. You don't need to wait until it expires. You can apply for a renewal up to six months beforehand. At the time of writing, renewing the card was free if you use the official website.

Note that EHIC cards issued after 2020 are not valid for use in the UK.

To get more details about how to apply for one, see the EHIC application for your country.

Useful sites

The EHIC & Brexit:

https://www.bbc.com/news/world-europe-44850972

Government healthcare advice for visitors to the UK from the EU:

https://www.gov.uk/guidance/healthcare-for-eu-and-efta-citizens-visiting-the-uk

Reciprocal healthcare arrangements for non-EU citizens:

https://www.nhs.uk/using-the-nhs/healthcare-abroad/healthcare-when-travelling-abroad/travelling-outside-the-european-economic-area-eea/

How to apply for a EHIC:

https://ec.europa.eu/social/main.jsp?catId=563

A selection of UK hospitals

These are not affiliate links. I do not necessarily know, like or trust any of these hospitals. They're for information only.

Hospitals in London:

Guys and St Thomas NHS Hospital

Institute of Cancer Research Royal Cancer Hospital

BMI Hospitals

Royal Marsden Hospital

South London and Maudsley NHS

North East London Mental Health NHS

Great Ormond Street Hospital

Chelsea and Westminster Hospital

University College London NHS Hospital

King's College NHS Hospital

Homerton University Hospital

St George's Healthcare Trust

London Bridge Hospital

Moorfields Eye Hospital

South West London and St George's Mental Health NHS Trust

Central and North West London Mental Health Trust

West London Mental Health NHS Trust

British Institute of Radiology

Hospitals in Birmingham:

Heart of England NHS Trust

University Hospital Birmingham NHS

Sandwell and West Birmingham NHS Hospital

Birmingham NHS Children's Hospital

Hospitals in Manchester:

Nuffield Hospital

Central Manchester University Hospital

Christies Hospital NHS

University Hospital of South Manchester

Salford Royal Hospital

Hospitals in Newcastle:

Nuffield Hospital

Newcastle-Upon-Tyne NHS Hospital

Royal Victoria Infirmary

Hospitals in Sheffield:

Sheffield NHS Teaching Hospital

BMI Thornbury Hospital

Royal Hallamshire Hospital

Hospitals in Liverpool:

Merseycare NHS

Royal Liverpool University Hospital

Clatterbridge Centre for Oncology NHS Trust

Hospitals in Bristol:

Nuffield Hospital

North Bristol NHS

University Hospital Bristol NHS

Hospitals in Edinburgh:

NHS Lothian

Royal Infirmary of Edinburgh

Royal Edinburgh Hospital

Hospitals in Glasgow

NHS Greater Glasgow and Clyde

BMI Ross Hall

Nuffield Hospital

Hospitals in Cardiff

Nuffield Health Cardiff Bay Hospital

University Hospital of Wales

Hospitals in Swansea

Sancta Maria Hospital Swansea

Singleton Hospital

Morriston Hospital

Hospitals in Belfast

Belfast City Hospital

Musgrave Park Hospital

Royal Jubilee Maternity Hospital

SECTION FOUR —
GETTING ABOUT

CHAPTER 13 —
Public Transportation

Introduction and purpose

The UK has a well-developed public transportation network in the larger towns and major centres. It's only when you get out to more rural towns that service can be patchy, at least in terms of frequency.

It is possible to fly from some cities, such as from London to Manchester or Edinburgh, but many people simply get the train for intercity journeys. The intercity train network is reasonable or good in many cases, despite what locals might have you believe.

Bus services

Within towns and cities, the bus seems to be the most common way of getting about and it can sometimes be cost effective. Some cities' bus networks (such as Reading) are operated as a not-for-profit scheme by the local government. Here are some things to bear in mind when taking the bus:

- As a rule, buses in larger towns and cities accept contactless methods of payment and some even require it. In London you can only use an Oyster card, which is a smart card used on London Transport and is a touch-on/touch-off system of paying.

- There is no need to touch off when exiting a bus in London but elsewhere it might be necessary. Check with the driver or conductor if in doubt.
- If you're under 18, or a full-time student, or if you're a pensioner, you can get concessionary fares. In some towns, seniors travel for free.
- Some vehicles are equipped with Wi-Fi on board.
- The buses don't run 24 hours, so if you're going to be out late, check the timetable to find out what time the last one leaves.

The Tube

Operated by TfL (Transport for London), the Tube is London's metro system (operating mostly underground but also above the surface in some places). The original network opened in the 1840's and has been continually modernised. The current network stretches far and wide, and over time it keeps expanding by adding new lines and new stations. If you're coming into or going out from Heathrow, the Tube has you covered from all Terminals.

The frequencies of trains are nothing short of legendary. In many cases, if you're in central London, you might only have to wait a minute for a train though the average wait time seems to be about 4 minutes.

Other cities that have a metro system are Newcastle, Glasgow and Liverpool.

Here are some things to bear in mind when taking the Tube:

- If you're arriving into Heathrow, the Tube is the cheapest way to travel into London. But the journey is quite long (at least half an hour).
- Think carefully about when to travel. During rush hour, you'll pay peak fares and trains can get very crowded.
- It's sometimes faster and easier to walk from one Tube station to another when getting about. TfL publishes maps and information about walking distances on their website.

Trains

Trains work well most of the time but intercity travel can be very expensive. An annual season ticket between London and a coastal Kentish town, for example, might cost several thousand pounds.

Services in different parts of the UK are operated by different companies, but on the whole, the services seem to integrate seamlessly. Most modern rolling stock now has carriages with toilets, Wi-Fi, and reserved seats for less mobile passengers. You may ordinarily occupy these seats but you must offer them up without being asked to move.

> ***Comment***: Try not to rely on train toilets. They're often out of service and sometimes a bit dirty.

If you plan to travel to/from Europe by train, the stations you would be travelling to (or from) would be Ashford (Kent), Ebbsfleet (Kent) and St. Pancras (London).

Some tips for train travel in the UK:

- Think about when you want to travel. There are different tickets for different times of day. Off-peak and super-offpeak are usually cheaper but you can't use them during peak hours. 'Anytime' tickets are more flexible.
- You're supposed to buy a ticket before boarding but in some cases this is not possible and you will then be expected to buy one on board from the inspector.
- If you're going to be travelling often, consider getting a Railcard. This will give you one-third off train fares.
- If you're travelling in to some cities like London, it might only show a destination of "London Terminals" on your ticket. This gives you flexibility of where in London to get off.

- If your train is cancelled or delayed, you might be eligible for a refund. Any ticket office, or the National Rail website will have information on this.

Trams

Trams are found only in a limited number of places such as Nottingham, Blackpool, Manchester and Edinburgh. They are a great way to get about the city. Be aware of trams when walking about the city. They don't make much noise and can come up on you unnoticed.

Coaches

An an alternative to using the train, coaches are available for intercity travel. Coaches are often much cheaper than the equivalent train service but unless you buy one of their more expensive flexible tickets, they give you much less flexibility, as I learned the hard way. If you buy an ordinary ticket, you'll have to pick specific coach departure times.

CASE STUDY:
Coach Travel – Learning the Hard Way

I once travelled to London on a day return trip and finished all my errands early, so I tried to get on an earlier return coach than my scheduled one, but they would not let me do so without having to buy a new ticket, or at least paying a surcharge. Basic coach tickets are valid only on particular services and this will be printed on your ticket. With National Express coaches, if you're uncertain of the exact times you're travelling, you can get a different type of ticket that gives more flexibility, but it costs more. But what I've found is if you do this, there is not much saving over a train ticket. After this experience, I vowed not to use coaches again. You might just as well get a train.

Comment: I feel much safer on a train than on a coach anyway. For one thing, the train and the network have built-in safety features. Secondly, there are no "non-professional" drivers on the train network. When you take a train, the only other vehicles on the network besides your train are *other* trains, and *all* trains are operated by highly trained and skilful drivers. But the coach? The driver of your coach might be very professional, but s/he still has to share the road with every Tom, Dick and Harry driver!

Taxis

Taxis are available everywhere and many towns and cities have several co-existing companies. Black cabs are a famous British icon. I recommend taking one at least once in your lifetime just for the experience. The interiors of these vehicles are surprisingly spacious and comfy. Their drivers are friendly and carry a wealth of knowledge. Black cabs can be hailed anywhere in the street. But normal taxis can be hired only by visiting a rank or calling a switchboard (or using an app). All taxis, minicabs and black cabs are supposed to be licensed.

Top tips for taxis:

- Never travel in an unlicensed vehicle.
- Taxis run on meters, so you can see the fare as you go. There may be other charges, such as for bridge or tunnel tolls, which get added on at the end of your journey.
- Tipping is not essential, what many people do is simply round it up to the nearest pound.
- If travelling to the airport, you can order your taxi ahead of time.

Comment: In the UK, taxi meters are fair and it's unlikely you'll ever find one with a rigged meter.

Comment: Uber is available throughout the UK. I believe the system is unfair for drivers and thus I do not recommend using Uber at all.

Airports

The UK has a number of international and many domestic airports. The latter provide essential travel for locals, serving many island communities. The busiest airports are London Heathrow and London Gatwick. London has four other smaller airports too – London City, London Stansted, Luton Airport and Southend Airport. You might use these when getting to and from Europe and Ireland.

Airports in the UK are maintained to high standards and they all have shopping and catering facilities. Only Heathrow and London City airports are represented on the Tube network. Getting to and from the other airports, you'd have to use the road or an overground train.

Cost structures have changed over time in the aviation industry in response to increasing competition. As a result, certain services are now considered chargeable extras. Examples of these might be checked luggage, onboard catering, onboard entertainment (Wi-Fi, movies etc.), and the ability to select a particular seat prior to boarding.

Public bike sharing

Public bike sharing schemes are now available in many cities and towns. The great thing is that by using these schemes your own bike is left at home, not out on the street where it can be vandalised or stolen. Bicycles don't create any pollution, can go where cars can't go and help you to get fit. If you're a tourist, they can be a great way to get about and quickly get to know a town or city. Public Bike Sharing (PBS) appeared in London a few years ago and since then other cities have started their own schemes. One of the most well-known schemes is the Santander Cycle Hire Scheme which is available in London, Swansea, Brunel and Milton Keynes.

Some employers have also set up their own private fleets of bikes just for their own staff to use.

If you're seriously interested in casual bike hire, check out Cycling UK. They've done a whole long article that goes into great detail, including which networks are available in which cities.

Lessons learned

1) The train is a great, if expensive, way to travel between cities. If you use it often, get a Railcard or a season ticket.
2) Licensed taxis are safe to use in the UK.
3) If travelling in London, an Oyster card is a must. These can be picked up at the airport, train stations and many retail outlets in London.

Useful sites

Transport for London:

https://tfl.gov.uk/modes/walking/

National Rail:

https://www.nationalrail.co.uk/default.aspx

Public Cycling Schemes:

https://www.cyclinguk.org/article/guide-hire-bikes-and-public-bike-share-schemes

CHAPTER 14 — *Driving in the UK*

Introduction and purpose

This chapter is not meant as an exhaustive guide to the rules of the road. The purpose of this chapter is to get you familiar with some of the basics and quirks of driving in the UK – stuff that might not be obvious. There should be enough information here for you to get by until such time as you have a proper chance to study the Highway Code. You will need to know about the Highway Code if you're going to be driving here long term.

Which side of the road?

If you're an American or European, we in the UK drive on the ~~wrong~~ left side of the road. And likewise, cars originally sold in the UK have their steering wheel on the opposite side too. In one book I read, the author was complaining that most of the cars are manual. There is a good choice of automatics available if you prefer them.

Pedestrian crossings

One thing I find fascinating is the way pedestrian (zebra) crossings are treated differently by motorists across the world.

In the UK, if a pedestrian is either on the crossing or waiting at the side, vehicles *must stop and allow them to cross. When you're the pedestrian, you may occasionally find motorists reluctant to stop but they're the exception. When you're the driver, make sure you yield to pedestrians.*

Traffic lights – sequencing

When you're sitting at the front of the queue waiting behind traffic lights, you might be thrown by the sequencing. I certainly was when I returned to the UK. I had actually completely forgotten about this. Before you see a green light, you always get red and amber appearing together. When you see this, it means "get ready to go" but you still have to wait for the green. This is a quintessentially British thing. You won't see this anywhere else in the world and if you do, you can be sure it's a former British colony.

> ***Comment***: Personally, I don't think this is really needed. It should be possible to go straight from red to green with no amber involved. But that is not how it's done in the UK. You'll get used to it.

You may not cross the line before the green light appears.

Turning at a red light

I'm aware that in the USA there is an implicit rule in all 50 states that says you're allowed to turn right after stopping at a red light. Keeping in mind that we drive on the other side in the UK, such a rule would translate as "Left turn on red permitted after stopping". In case you're wondering, there is no such rule here. You may *not* turn left on a red light, unless there is a sign indicating otherwise or you have a green light pointing left.

Road markings – what do they all mean?

There are many road markings and they all mean something. It's obvious what some of them mean. For a comprehensive list of them, please refer to https://theorypass.co.uk/highway-code/road-markings/

***Insider Tip*: A hack for converting yards to metres**

Yards are used on some road signs in the UK. What are yards? If you're comfortable with yards, feel free to skip this tip. But if like me you're bemused by yards, read on.

If you're on a highway or motorway in the UK, short distances are often posted in yards. This might be the case if for example there is a sign telling you the distance remaining to the next junction, roadworks, lane merge etc.

There is a very easy way to convert yards to metres, and you can do it in your head while sitting at the wheel as long as your mental arithmetic is not too shabby.

For example, when I see a sign telling me there are roadworks in 800 yards, I cannot gauge the distance in front of me. I mean I know intuitively that a yard is just over 91 cm, but that doesn't help me.

To convert to metres, this is the approach I use. I divide the number by 10 (just drop the last digit). In this example, dropping the last digit of 800 gives 80. Then I simply subtract this number from the original number (800 yards). This gives 800-80 = 720. That means the distance is approximately 720 m. It's not precisely the same as 800 yards, but it's near enough.

Petrol prices

I'm sorry, I don't have much good news for you in this section, and you've probably already guessed what it is! Petrol (gas) is priced by the litre (liter) and prices are in the range £1.00 to £1.30 per litre. That's about double what you can expect to pay at most places in Australia and about triple the expected prices in America. If you're from America, how does the idea of paying US$6 per US gallon grab you?...I know, it's painful. But you'll get used to it. Most of this, of course, is government duties and taxes. Look on the bright side – you're helping to finance new schools and hospitals.

> ***Comment***: Check your app store to see what apps are available to help you find the least expensive petrol prices in your area. There should be plenty of apps to guide you.

> ***Insider Tip***: If you're grappling with the idea of a litre, a litre is slightly more than one US quart. One litre equates to one quart plus two fluid ounces.

Is your driving licence valid in the UK?

If you already hold a driving licence obtained in another country, it is usually valid for 12 months in the UK. There is a tool available to verify whether you're allowed to drive in the UK on your foreign licence.

If your licence is not valid for use in the UK, or if you've been resident in the UK for longer than 12 months, you must obtain a British licence. This is achieved by passing a theory test followed by a practical test. Taking these tests is not necessary for everyone. If you obtained your foreign licence in a "designated country", a concession is available to you: You can simply go ahead and "exchange" your licence for a British one by filling in a simple form and paying a nominal fee. This means, you don't need to take any tests. If you go ahead and answer the questions in the tool, you can see if your country is on the designated list.

Lessons learned

1) In the UK we drive on the left hand side of the road.
2) You must wait for pedestrians on zebra crossings.

3) Beware the traffic light sequencing might not be what you're used to when going from red to green. You may not cross the line until you get a green.

4) If you want to save money on petrol, try an app from your app store.

5) For most people, their existing foreign driving licence is valid in the UK for the first 12 months of residency. After that, they can simply get a British licence after filling in a form and paying a fee. Some drivers will need to take formal tests before they're granted a UK licence.

Useful sites

The Highway Code (rules of the road):

https://www.gov.uk/browse/driving/highway-code-road-safety

Driving in the UK on a foreign licence:

https://www.gov.uk/driving-nongb-licence

Driving test theory:

https://www.gov.uk/driving-theory-test

Practical driving test:

https://www.gov.uk/practical-driving-test-for-cars

SECTION FIVE — FINDING YOUR ACCOMMODATION

CHAPTER 15 — *Renting*

Introduction and purpose

In this chapter, I will discuss the advantages and disadvantages of renting and then outline a few of the places you can search to find a place to stay.

Renting – advantages and disadvantages

Renting is great if you're unsure of where you'd like to stay and you want to "try out" an area before you commit to it long term. In major cities like London you can easily find short-term leases with short notice periods. You don't have to worry about repairs or maintenance in a rental property.

The main downside to renting is that you don't have ultimate control over your property. The landlord can give you notice, for example, of cancelling the contract and getting you to move (this is unlikely unless you're a "bad" tenant). But there can be other issues such as repair requests being ignored. It's times like these that it can be beneficial having a rental agreement in place. If you've rented a property through an agent, they will want to do everything by the book and you will have a proper contract setting out your rights and what's expected of you. With an agent involved, you will have more leverage over a landlord.

Then there's the issue they might want to sell it to another landlord (or to anyone else). In that case, you'll face the inconvenience of having strangers walking around your home inspecting it, though you should receive some warning in advance whenever somebody wants to inspect the property.

Another disadvantage is that you may not make any changes to the property. Sure, you might be allowed to re-arrange the furniture (if it's supplied as a furnished property), but I'm talking about painting the walls or adding new fittings and so on. You won't be able to re-decorate it.

Also be aware that when renting through an agent, it is likely they will do a background credit check against you. After all, by signing a contract, you're effectively entering into a credit arrangement even though you're paying the rent in advance.

Options for renting

Short term rentals can be found on Airbnb, MagicStay, Homeaway, TripAdvisor, Gumtree or Booking. Short term rentals are casual in that there is no contract to sign and the places usually come furnished.

Then of course, there's the standard hotel room and bed & breakfast place which is arguably the most expensive of all the options, but it's the most casual. There are so many different sites where you can search for these and I'm sure you have a few favourite sites of your own but in case you don't, there's Skiplagged, Expedia, Trip Advisor, Wotif and many more. By the way, Skiplagged often has very competitive airfares as well.

For less casual accommodation, try Right Move. Here, you can search by city, town and even post code. If you're a student, they also have a section for student properties to let. Be aware that these listings are specifically aimed at students meaning that you will literally be renting just one room in a shared house. They sometimes even specify "students only" in the wording of the ad and there will often be other restrictive conditions such as no children/pets etc.

There is usually no contract or credit check performed for short term rentals. You simply need to be a member of the platform and to have a form of government-issued photo ID.

Short term rentals – expected rates

As such, short term rentals cover stays under six months in duration while medium term rentals cover 6-12 month tenancies. Your circumstances might dictate you cannot sign a 6-month or 12-month lease.

This is when a short-term rental would be handy. The Residential Landlords Association gives the average nightly rent of an Airbnb London home as £137 (US$177). The median for long term rentals in London is £1700 (US$2205) per month which would give an average nightly rent of £56 (US$72).

Renting a house or apartment

This section covers formal renting, usually with a contract. Knowing exactly how to rent in the UK is vital. There are a great variety of properties available and price variation is enormous depending on where you rent. When deciding on where and what to rent, you'll need to take into account not just your budget but convenience for shopping and commuting, and what the area is like. This process can be initiated even before you arrive in the UK.

A rental will be your best bet if you plan to come to the UK temporarily. You could for example start with a short-term rental, then take something with a contract for 6 months or longer. Your landlord will look after repairs and maintenance. They have a duty of care to ensure your home is habitable and safe. Landlords are responsible for:

- The condition of the structure and exterior of the property including the roof

- Gutters, drains and pipes
- Wiring, central heating & fixed appliances e.g. cookers
- Hot water appliances.

Expected rents

Rents are usually quoted per calendar month (pcm). What you pay will vary enormously depending on what you rent and where. The national average is around £1000 (US$1300) pcm but in Greater London, you might only be able to get a studio flat for that much money. A two-bedroom flat in Greater London could fetch £1500 pcm or it could be as high as £2000 pcm or more if you want 3 bedrooms. It is possible to get a 4-bedroom place for under £2000 but it will be basic. At the top end of the scale, a 5-bedroom detached house might go for £5000-£10,000 pcm.

How to rent a property

Once you've decided on a specific property, you'll need to sign the contract and pay a security deposit (usually a month's rent). Sometimes, the landlord is open to negotiation on the rent, so it's worth checking before you sign. Read the contract carefully before you sign. You might be asked for some or all of the following:

- Government-issued photo ID;

- Evidence of visa;
- Payslips or bank statement showing receipt of earnings;
- Letter from your employer confirming employment details and/or employment contract;
- References from previous landlord(s).

Rental contract and deposit

At a minimum, your rental contract should set out the following details:

- Your name and your landlord's name and contact details;
- Address of the property being leased;
- The start date and duration of the term;
- How much rent is due, and when;
- Dates and frequency of rental inspections;
- Details of your security deposit and conditions to be met for getting it back;
- Deposit protection scheme (the landlord has a legal obligation to place your deposit into a DPS).
- Who is responsible for maintenance and repairs;
- Subletting policy;

- Other special conditions and fees.

There will be an inventory report listing items which are present from the start of your tenancy. Check that these items are really there before you move in, otherwise you will be liable for them. Also check that any pre-existing damage has been noted on the condition report. The cost of making good any damage during your term will be deducted from your security deposit.

Paying bills

As a tenant, you will be responsible for paying for water usage, electricity and gas consumption. You will need to open accounts in your own name for the last two. I have full details for how to do this in Chapter 21 – *Signing up for Gas and Electricity*.

Your rights as a tenant

When you rent a property, you have the following rights:

- The right to live in a property which is safe and fit for dwelling;
- The right to know who your landlord is;
- The right to view the Energy Performance Certificate (EPC) for the property. This is a

document required for properties when they're constructed, sold or let. It tells you the energy efficiency of a property, and is a grade from A (most efficient) to G (least efficient). For a rented property, this usually needs to be at least an E.

- The right to utilise the property in peace, undisturbed.
- The right to be protected from unfair eviction and excessive rent increases.
- The right to not have to pay certain fees when establishing a new tenancy.

Any tenancy agreement you have should be fair and legal. The landlord(s) must identify themselves to you within 21 days, or they risk being fined.

As a tenant, the rights outlined above come with a few responsibilities. You will be expected to:

- Make every reasonable effort to keep the property in a good state, and not cause any damage.
- Promptly pay all bills and charges for which you are liable.
- Pay your rent on time, even if repairs are pending and/or you're involved in a dispute. You may not withhold rent under these circumstances.

- Turn off the main water supply to the property if you're going to be away during winter.

The Government has a full page with very detailed information on rights and responsibilities.

Renting privately

When you rent privately, this means there is no agent involved – you deal directly with the landlord. You will still have the same legal rights, protections and responsibilities and you should still have a contract, for your own safety.

Lesson learned

1) Renting gives you convenience and flexibility. As a tenant, you have both rights and responsibilities.
2) You don't need to pay for maintenance but you do need to pay for the bills.
3) For your protection, your rental should have a written agreement.

Useful sites

https://www.rightmove.co.uk/property-to-rent.html

https://www.gumtree.com/property-to-rent

https://www.gumtree.com/property-to-share

Renting

https://www.airbnb.com/

https://www.magicstay.com/

https://skiplagged.com/

https://www.expedia.com/

https://www.tripadvisor.com/

https://www.wotif.com/

https://www.gov.uk/government/publications/landlord-and-tenant-rights-and-responsibilities-in-the-private-rented-sector

https://www.gov.uk/private-renting

CHAPTER 16 —
Introduction to Buying a Home

Introduction and purpose

So you've been renting for a while and you're sick of paying rent. Or you think it's cheaper to make mortgage payments over a property which will eventually become your own place outright when the loan is paid off. Or perhaps you're really brave and you want to dive in at the deep end immediately, not spending any time as a tenant. The next step up is to buy a place of your own. That's what this chapter is all about. Here, I'll explain the basics of buying a home and what to look out for.

Pros and cons of buying your own home

So first of all, what are the pros and cons of purchasing your own property?

First and most obviously, you have total control. The property is your own and you may renovate it as you see fit. If you don't like the interior, you can give it a full makeover. Same with the outside (subject to council approval, if needed). The flip side of this is that as the owner, you are your own landlord so you are responsible for maintenance, repairs and insurance. Speaking of landlords, after you've purchased, you'll never have to worry about routine landlord or agent inspections (you might occasionally get a TV licence inspector – more on this in the chapter about television).

If you've bought a property in a good and sought-after area, there's a good chance your home will appreciate in value over time but property prices in the UK can go up or down so there is the possibility that the value of your home, in the short term at least, could go backwards.

One definite downside of buying your own place is that if you find you have bad neighbours (or your relationship with them sours for some reason), you are effectively stuck with them until you sell or they move out first.

Other things to consider when buying

Internet speeds

Imagine you've spent weeks or months finding the perfect house in the perfect location, only to move in, connect to the internet and find the speeds are terrible. Before buying a property (or renting one for that matter), it's a good idea to check the expected data speeds at that location. OpenReach are the company responsible for the network infrastructure. They have a handy tool on their site which can give you an idea of speeds to expect at any address. All you need to do is plug in the post code of the address where you're thinking of moving to and then select the property number. It will then tell you what speeds you can expect. If you're really lucky, you will have "fibre to the premises" (fttp) which offer the best speeds. Most addresses do not enjoy fttp yet.

You should also check the performance of mobile internet. This is very easy to do – visit speedtest on your mobile device when you go to inspect the property. Also check how well your favourite websites perform while you're in the property. While inspecting the property, try to do some of the things you usually do at home on your smartphone or tablet, including calling and messaging. This will give you an idea of mobile data reception there.

Cost of living

If you pick a capital city or main centre, you can of course expect to pay higher prices for a given property. But in many cases, those places with higher property prices often have lower living costs. It's worth factoring in the cost of living in the city or town you're considering.

Proximity of schools, shops & transportation

How convenient the place you are considering buying is useful to know not just for yourself but also for re-saleability purposes. In other words, a property close to all the most useful facilities will be easier to sell in the future.

Weather-prone areas

Certain parts of the UK are susceptible to flooding, and others suffer more when there are nationwide gales. Property prices might be lower in these areas but if your home is damaged by the weather, it will cause you inconvenience, not to mention a nuisance to chase up the insurance company.

Job opportunities

If you are going to be a company employee and you are unable to work from home, it's likely your job will have some bearing over the location where you choose to buy. Having said this, many people who work in London don't live near London at all. They commute to and from work in the morning and evening. This allows them to live in a less expensive property but there is still the cost of commuting which can be high.

Crime rates

This might not be a consideration for everyone, but I think it's worth at least a cursory look. There is probably no such thing as a crime-free area anywhere but you should be aware of what to expect. There are tools online to get an idea of what crime rates are like and if you know the post code of where you plan to live, crime statistics can tell you about reported crime rates in a given street. But don't rely just on online tools. Visit the street and the surrounding areas at random times of the day and evening. What kinds of people pass through those areas or hang out there? Is there much graffiti around? How much litter is on the ground? And can you see any cars missing their wheels and standing on bricks? Can you see properties in poor states of repair? These are tell-tale signs of "bad" areas. On the flip side, it's reasonable to assume that high(er) crime areas will have lower property prices.

Lessons learned

1) You should consider buying a property if you plan to stay medium to long term in the UK and you can afford to do so.

2) There are many factors to consider when choosing a location. Among them are cost of living, expected broadband speeds, local facilities and crime rates.

Useful sites

https://www.speedtest.net/

https://www.openreach.com/fibre-broadband/

http://www.numbeo.com/cost-of-living/country_result.jsp?country=United+Kingdom

https://crime-statistics.co.uk/

CHAPTER 17 — *Bonus: The Complete Guide to Mortgages and Buying a Home*

This is a bonus chapter. If you've not already done so, go ahead and pick up your bonus chapters from https://easyukmigration.com/bookbonus

You only have to do this once, and you will get all the bonuses for this book together in one email.

SECTION SIX — DOMESTIC MATTERS

CHAPTER 18 — *Connecting Broadband, TV & Telephone*

Introduction and purpose

This chapter discusses various internet service providers (ISPs) including how they are rated.

Broadband, telephone and TV – a quick rundown of ISPs

Internet service providers (ISPs) these days will deal with both internet and telephony products (fixed line and mobiles) and often, TV services too. As with the energy providers, once again the top performers, according to *Which?* consumer service are actually the smaller companies which relatively few people have heard of. Yes, you need to be a member to see the actual results of that report, but I'll save you the trouble and will give you the salient results here.

According to that report, Zen Internet is the top provider with a customer score of 84%.

> ***Comment***: I have been with Zen for over a year and am more than happy with them. I've never had a problem with them.

Best of all, their entire outfit is in the UK. They are not only headquartered in the UK but have a UK-based customer support centre too. That means by using their services, you're supporting the UK economy.

In second place is Utility Warehouse with a customer score of 70%. Curiously, they are the only *Which?* recommended provider.

PlusNet, with a score of 65%, has some very good value deals and they come a close third place.

Once again, as with energy providers, the big names are actually the laggards. Sky, BT, Talk Talk and Virgin Media all fall in the bottom half of the ratings table, with customer scores ranging from 55% to 59%.

Comment: Before moving to Zen, I had some particularly bad customer support experience with BT, with my calls always landing in a faraway country, being passed from one person to another, and many of these support staff speaking with thick accents that are sometimes barely understandable. In the end, after I left them, they were tripping over themselves to get me back, contacting me on no fewer than five separate occasions to win back my custom with all kinds of sweet talk and great sounding deals. They even wanted to buy me out of my new contract. All their efforts were in vain.

Broadband speeds: setting expectations

Depending on where you come from, you might be accustomed to broadband speeds of hundreds of Mbps or even gigabit speeds. For the most part download speeds are very modest in the UK so don't expect blindingly fast download speeds. A typical household can expect from 30 Mbps to 80 Mbps. Only Virgin Media (which is available only in select areas) offers respectable speeds. With Virgin, you can expect speeds upwards of 100 Mbps, and potentially up to 300 Mbps.

To get a good idea of what speeds to expect at your new address, use the OpenReach tool. Then plug in the post code of the address to where you're moving and select your address from the dropdown box. It will tell you what wired speeds are available at that address.

Regulation of service providers

The body that regulates the conduct of companies providing TV, radio, video, phone and broadband services is Ofcom. They take decisions on price controls and enforcement, and act in the interests of consumers.

Useful sites

Service provider ratings:

https://www.which.co.uk/reviews/broadband-deals/article/best-broadband-providers

Comparison sites for broadband, telephone & mobile and content:

https://switch.which.co.uk/

https://www.comparethemarket.com/

Check broadband speeds:

https://www.openreach.com/fibre-broadband/

CHAPTER 19 —
Signing up for Water Supply

Introduction and purpose

This chapter describes how to register with a water supplier.

Water supply

If you're a tenant renting a property, the water will usually already be connected and an account will already be active before you even move in. What you need to do is check who is responsible for paying the water bill – whether the landlord or yourself. If water usage is not covered in your tenancy agreement, then the water account will be transferred to your name.

If you've purchased your own home, you should identify your local supplier. You will need the post code of the property into which you are moving. Once you've identified the relevant supplier for your area, visit their website for information on how to open a new account. You will pay two charges on your water bill – one for water supplied and another for waste water disposal.

Water faults

If you're having difficulties with your water supply, you should contact your local authority. You can find the contact details on water bills or on the company website. To find an approved plumber including emergency plumbers, contact WaterSafe.

Complaints about water

If you're unable to resolve a complaint or dispute with your water supplier, you can escalate it to the Consumer Council for Water in England and Wales, or the Scottish Public Services Ombudsman in Scotland.

Useful sites

Find the water supplier for your area:

https://www.water.org.uk/advice-for-customers/find-your-supplier/

Water faults:

https://www.watersafe.org.uk/

Complaints that cannot be resolved:

https://www.ccwater.org.uk/make-a-complaint/ (England & Wales)

https://www.spso.org.uk/ (Scotland)

CHAPTER 20 —
Electricity

Introduction & purpose

This chapter contains important background information about the electricity supply in the UK. Many expats get rid of their electrical appliances before moving to the UK and then get new ones after they arrive. That's perfectly fine. Whether you do this or not, there is information in this chapter that's still necessary to know.

Electricity standards

The standard electrical supply in the UK is 230V AC at 50Hz. Provided you have a plug adaptor, appliances from overseas will work just fine in the UK unless the appliances you're bringing are from Canada, the USA, Latin America, the Caribbean and a handful of other countries like Taiwan and Japan. All appliances used in UK households must have a fuse. If any device you bring doesn't have a fuse, it will need an approved plug adaptor.

Plug type & socket

The UK uses what is known as plug Type G. Pictured here are a UK socket and plug.

If you are coming from Ireland, Malta, Cyprus, Hong Kong, Singapore, Malaysia, Sri Lanka, parts of Africa, parts of the Middle East and British Overseas Territories, you won't need a plug adaptor as long as your device has a fuse in the plug.

Supply reliability

The electrical supply in the UK is very reliable and outages are practically unheard of. The uptime in the supply to your home can be measured in years if not decades. If there is an outage, it is often weather-related.

Which appliances should you bring?

If you're coming from the Americas or Japan, the following items are best left behind: large appliances such as cinema-style TVs, fridges and washing machines, kitchen appliances, hair dryers, hair straighteners and clothes irons. These devices are not usually designed for worldwide use and plugging them into a UK socket will result in a big bang and/or a puff of smoke from your appliance!

On the other hand, most modern consumer electronic devices such as notebook power supplies and phone chargers are of course designed to be used worldwide.

How can you tell if a device can be used worldwide without a voltage convertor? Devices which are designed for worldwide use are usually labelled with an input of 100-240V and can therefore be safely plugged in anywhere in the world without a voltage convertor, including the UK. As long as the higher number is at least 220V, it's fine to use in the UK. Here's an example of what to look for:

What plug adaptor to get

Pictured below is an example of a safe and approved adaptor. If the plug design of your device is Type G, you shouldn't need an adaptor. I say "shouldn't" because not all Type G plugs contain a fuse. All household appliances plugged into UK mains MUST incorporate a fuse in the circuit. Therefore, if the plug on your device does not contain any fuse, you will need to get a plug adaptor with a fuse.

WARNING! Always check that your device is compatible with the household electrical supply before plugging it in! In other words, the voltage must match up.

WARNING! Plug adaptors do NOT convert voltage. They merely allow your device to be physically plugged into a wall socket, that's all.

One plug adaptor to avoid

Be cautious when selecting a plug adaptor. Not all plug adaptors are suitable for use in the UK. An example of a dangerous adaptor is shown below. This video explains why the plug adaptor pictured here is dangerous. You can expect this type of adaptor to be sold from unscrupulous or shady online traders (some of whom are third-party traders who operate on Amazon & eBay). Beware.

Dangerous plug adaptor. DO NOT USE!

Safety covers for sockets

In many countries and in the UK, some parents buy socket covers to place over unused sockets in order to prevent small children from inserting anything into the terminals. But with a UK style socket, safety covers are neither necessary nor desirable and could even be dangerous. Here is a good video which explains everything.

Useful references

Important safety information:

http://youtu.be/d-WhFgaqCX0

https://youtu.be/jUu8a6MP0iI

CHAPTER 21 —
Signing up for Gas & Electricity

Introduction and purpose

The purpose of this chapter is to help you with selecting and signing up for an energy provider.

This is the only chapter in the book that contains an affiliate link. There is just one affiliate link in this chapter. If you use it to sign up to this particular provider, I will benefit, but so will you. I would not recommend something I myself don't use or that I would not use. I both use and recommend this particular provider.

The energy market

The energy (gas and electricity) market in the UK is privatised. This means you have a choice of which retailer to use for your energy needs. In fact, if you wanted, you could choose to have your electricity and gas accounts with separate providers although for convenience, many customers use one provider to get both their electricity and gas. There are a number of online tools to help you decide which company to choose. One such tool is switch.which.co.uk. This is a tool provided by *Which?* consumer organisation. They are the foremost consumer organisation and are renowned for their impartiality. One alternative comparison site for energy providers is www.ukpower.co.uk which is a government-backed site. You can use these tools even if you're new to the UK energy market (meaning you have no existing provider).

There are over 50 energy suppliers in the UK, so you have plenty of choice! Out of these 50 companies, six companies control 70% of the market share between them. The interesting thing is that according to a recent *Which?* consumer survey of more than 8000 customers, these same six companies were rated near the bottom of the table in terms of overall customer satisfaction. Why customers choose to remain with them is a mystery but I can only guess it's either ignorance or rank complacency in putting up with unsatisfactory service.

The *Which?* survey evaluates energy companies based on the following criteria: Bill accuracy, bill clarity, customer service, complaints handling, digital tools and value for money.

Which? uses a set of stringent criteria for deciding which companies to recommend. According to these criteria, there are only three energy companies that come with the coveted *Which? Recommended Provider* (WRP) badge. This is not something they give out lightly. In February 2020, these companies along with their respective customer scores were identified as Octopus Energy (83%), Pure Planet (78%) and So Energy (75%). These companies punch above their weight.

Selecting an energy provider (or switching your energy provider to a different one) is a trivial process. (You don't need to wait until you move house, you can do it anytime.) Among the main reasons people switch providers are price increases (especially unannounced ones), direct debit problems and inaccurate billing or meter reading.

For some customers, picking the provider with the cheapest prices is the only thing that matters. But this might not be the best thing for you in the long run. In the preceding paragraph, I've touched on some of the problems you might encounter when price is your only consideration.

Safety and emergencies

When you move in to a property, you should familiarise yourself with the locations of your gas tap and electricity consumer unit so you know where they are for emergencies. If you smell gas, you should shut off the gas immediately, open all doors and windows (even if it's the middle of winter). **Do not turn on or off any electrical appliances.** Call the gas emergency number which is 0800 111 999. Use a mobile and make the call only when you're well outside of the house.

If you run a business or have a rental property, you are legally obliged to have all gas appliances checked annually by a registered technician. Do not attempt any repairs yourself. Doing so is illegal and dangerous.

For electrical repairs, you will need to find an electrical competent person.

How energy billing usually works

Most companies prefer you to be billed by direct debit. Under direct debit, you agree to allow the company to take pre-agreed amounts of money directly from your bank account to cover your energy bills. This is good for you because it helps to eliminate bill shock. (Instead of one big bill every quarter, payments are spread out, usually one per month, to cover your energy bill.) It's also good for the company because it facilitates their cash flow.

Octopus Energy – what makes it so great?

As I mentioned above, *Octopus Energy* is not just a *Which?* Recommended Provider of energy. It was crowned the top energy provider for the second year in a row in 2020 and maintains its *Which?* Recommended Provider status for the third consecutive year.

I use *Octopus Energy* because of the user-friendliness of their online account interface and the amount of functionality built into it. For example, they have even given the customer the power to amend their direct debit amounts (up or down) and change the date of payment.

Some of the things that really impressed me were the quick and painless sign-up process and also the fact that they did not take any money from me before my official start date with them. Some energy providers charge you an exit fee to leave but with Octopus there is no exit fee on any of their plans. You can come and go anytime without penalty.

What's more, they source 100% of their electricity from renewable sources (one of the few companies that does this), so you're doing your bit for the environment. (This doesn't mean that the electricity coming into your home is necessarily all from renewable sources. It just means that for the electricity you do use, an equivalent amount of electricity from renewable sources has been pumped back into the grid by Octopus.)

How to make £50 free money

Now for the juicy bit. When you sign up with Octopus Energy, they will split £100 between you and me. You will receive your £50 bonus sign-up credit after your account has been opened and your direct debit is active. To open your account and claim your free £50 bonus credit, simply click on https://share.octopus.energy/storm-leaf-177 or enter it into your browser if you're reading the paperback version of this book. There are no catches. You'll be using electricity one way or another, so you might as well take advantage of this. Just to be clear, I will benefit from this financially, but so will you.

When you click on the link above, this is what you should see on your screen:

How to get free energy indefinitely

When you sign up with Octopus Energy, you will automatically be assigned your own unique affiliate link. You can then share this out to your friends, family, neighbours or whoever. One customer has even created a side-hustle out of this. He's made thousands in affiliate commissions with Octopus Energy just by using his affiliate link. Needless to say, he's got free energy indefinitely because of all the affiliate commissions he's earned.

Now I know what you're probably wondering. What about saturation? Well, let's remember that currently Octopus Energy holds under 5% of the entire energy market. This means out of 20 random householders you meet on the street, 19 of them are *not* with Octopus Energy so there is an enormous potential to earn affiliate income here. You just need to get creative with how you do it. As an example, you could create a blog and cite your affiliate link there.

What about Northern Ireland?

Octopus covers only Great Britain (that's England, Wales and Scotland) and does not extend to Northern Ireland. But the good news is the *Which?* consumer report has cited six suppliers for Northern Ireland. None of them is a *Which?* Recommended Provider but they did all score above 60% as an overall customer score which is not too shabby. Best first, they are Electric Ireland, Budget Energy, Power NI, Firmus Energy, SSE Airtricity Gas and SSE Airtricity Elec.

Complaints about energy

You should make every effort to resolve any issues or disputes you have with your energy provider(s) direct with the supplier. If you find you're getting nowhere, you can escalate your complaint to the Energy Ombudsman.

Lessons learned

1) The energy market is privatised in the UK and there is a big choice of companies.
2) The "big 6" are near the bottom of the rankings according to leading consumer service *Which?*
3) The same survey identifies the top providers as Octopus Energy, Pure Planet and So Energy.
4) When you move into a new property, locate the gas tap and the electricity consumer unit so you know where to go to shut off supplies in an emergency.
5) If you sign up to Octopus Energy using my affiliate link https://share.octopus.energy/storm-leaf-177 you will get £50 automatically credited to your energy account. I use and recommend Octopus Energy. You can then get your own referral link and start earning affiliate income.

Useful sites

Get a bonus £50 credited to your energy account:

https://share.octopus.energy/storm-leaf-177

Comparison sites for utilities:

https://switch.which.co.uk/

www.ukpower.co.uk

Energy ombudsman (for complaints that cannot be resolved):

https://www.ombudsman-services.org/

For technical assistance:

https://www.gassaferegister.co.uk/

http://www.electricalcompetentperson.co.uk/

Gas emergencies:

Freephone 0800 111 999

CHAPTER 22 —
Signing up for Other Domestic Services

Introduction and purpose

This chapter discusses other services you need to arrange when moving into a new property.

Council taxes

Council taxes are levied on every property, at the property level. These cover public services such as refuse collection, recycling collection, cleaning and public maintenance. Some councils will give you a discount if you're in a one-person household. To check how much council tax you will pay, and to register, simply visit the government council tax bands web site. You will be directed to the appropriate council web site based on the post code you enter.

Insurance

Last but not least, is your insurance bill. Insurance covers you against fire, theft and flooding. Insurance is not compulsory but is a good idea to have. If you're in rented accommodation, you need only bother with contents insurance. This will cover only your possessions. If you're living in a property you purchased, you should get both building and contents insurance. This will cover your possessions as well as unexpected damage to the property.

As always, *Which?* can point out the providers who are good and the ones to avoid.

Are you feeling overwhelmed?

In the last few chapters, we've covered a whole cartload of things you need to do when moving to a new address. You have to connect your gas, electricity, internet/phone and mobile services. Then you have to register for water billing and council taxes, not to mention arrange insurance.

If you're overwhelmed and stressed out by all of the above, I can totally understand. Fortunately, there is a service which can take care of all of the above on your behalf. Please connect me can deal with *everything* when moving into a new property. They can arrange for your gas, electricity, internet/telephone, water connection, council tax registration and insurance.

It's important to point out that I don't have any personal experience of using them, nor do I have any feedback about how good they are, other than the testimonials they've put on their site. Therefore, I'm not affiliated with them, nor am I recommending them. I'm merely drawing your attention to their existence. Having said that, I have no reason to doubt their capability or reliability. All I'm saying is use them at your own risk.

Useful sites

Find your local council (registering for council tax):

https://www.gov.uk/council-tax-bands

Comparison sites for insurance:

https://switch.which.co.uk/

https://www.comparethemarket.com/

A service which connects all your utilities and more:

https://pleaseconnectme.co.uk/

CHAPTER 23 —
Home Entertainment: TV & Radio

Introduction and purpose

Television has come a long way in the last 20 years. When I left the UK to move abroad, there were literally just four channels – BBC1, BBC2, ITV and Channel 4. So imagine my surprise when I returned recently to find an overwhelming choice of not only terrestrial channels but also satellite services, not to mention on-demand streaming services. It's also possible to access content which is from other countries. I'll discuss that towards the end of the chapter.

The purpose of this chapter is to outline what's available and how to get it.

TV licence

To watch TV in the UK, you must buy a licence. At the time of writing, an annual licence for a colour TV cost £157.50. This covers all BBC content, some other national and regional TV channels plus a host of radio services. The most up-to-date-prices can be found here. There is also clear information on the TV licensing site to outline the circumstances under which you need a licence. Consuming TV content without a licence attracts a large fine and possible prosecution. "You need a licence" seems to be the default attitude of these people. In other words, if caught without a licence, the onus will be on you to prove you don't need one. If you don't have an actual TV set but you do have a content-capable device like a laptop or tablet for example, they will argue you do need a licence.

Terrestrial channels

Terrestrial channels are now all digital. They can be accessed through Freeview. Instead of Freeview, there is also Freesat which is available through satellite. You will need a modern, digital TV for this and a good antenna. The main broadcasters are BBC, ITV, Channel 4, Channel 5 and UKTV (part of the BBC). All of them operate multiple channels.

There is also regional TV, which is available only in certain places. Among these are London Live, S4C (Welsh language programming), That's Manchester and BBC Alba (Scottish Gaelic).

Satellite and cable TV

Those who subscribe to satellite and cable TV usually do so in a way which is bundled with their home broadband service and/or telephony services. The usual content providers are Virgin Media, Talk Talk, Sky and BT. Taking out a satellite/cable TV package will give you access to many more channels such as live international sport and entertainment. There are also on-demand streaming services and interactive TV.

The choice is vast and these providers allow you to customise what's included in your subscription. To help you navigate the market, try a comparison site like confused.com.

International TV

International TV is available but you'll need to take out some kind of satellite/cable TV subscription. There is another way, which I'll discuss in the next chapter.

Radio services

The BBC operates radio services in English, Welsh and Scottish Gaelic and broadcasting is both analogue and digital. You don't need a radio, of course, a smartphone can be used and you can also use your digital TV/ Freeview to receive radio programmes. There are stations dedicated to different genres of music as well as news. There are also local radio stations.

Useful sites

https://www.freeview.co.uk/

https://www.tvlicensing.co.uk/check-if-you-need-one

https://www.tvlicensing.co.uk/check-if-you-need-one/topics/tv-licence-types-and-costs-top2

Comparison sites for cable & satelliteTV:

https://www.confused.com/

CHAPTER 24 — *Bonus: How to Access International TV*

CHAPTER 25 — *Bonus: How to Deal with Tradespeople*

Chapters 24 & 25 are bonus chapters. If you've not already done so, go ahead and pick up your bonus chapters from https://easyukmigration.com/bookbonus

You only have to do this once, and you will get all the bonuses for this book together in one email.

SECTION SEVEN — EDUCATION, BUSINESS & WORK

CHAPTER 26 — *Childcare in the UK*

Introduction and purpose

If you have young children, you'll be pleased to know childcare is easily accessible and there are some great options. The purpose of this chapter is to outline them and give you an idea of costs.

Options for childcare

Day Nursery. The UK has community, council, workplace and private day nurseries. They are regulated by Ofsted (Office of Standards in Education – a Government department that inspects facilities providing education and skills for learners of all ages) or the Care and Social Services Inspectorate Wales (CSSIW). Day nurseries offer a full day service for children under 5 years of age.

Childminders. A childminder is a self-employed child carer who works out of her own home. It's a good idea to think about and negotiate hours, rates, terms and conditions before signing an agreement. The prices will vary depending on how old your child is and which region you're in. Childminders are inspected by the same bodies who regulate day nurseries.

Nanny/Au-pair. If a more personalised service is what you want, consider a nanny or au-pair. The advantage of this is that your child need not leave the house and will remain in a comfortable and familiar environment. But this is a double-edged sword in that s/he might not get the opportunity for vital interaction with his/her own peers. A nanny might charge from £300 to £500 per week, and tax and national insurance would be on top. Your nanny should be part of the Ofsted voluntary childcare register or Childcare Approval Scheme in Wales. If not, the onus falls on you to do due diligence including background checks and following up on references.

Children's centres. Child centres operate all year round and their hours will be something like 8 AM to 6 PM. You don't need to leave your child there the whole day – you can pick the hours that are best for you. Details of child centres can be found on your local family information services website.

Other options. Some pre-school facilities offer part time child care. These are suitable for children of ages 3-5. There are play groups, early education nursery classes and out-of-school services. Out-of-school facilities might have things like a holiday play scheme for the school holidays, an after school club or even just a breakfast club before school. You can expect to pay up to £100 per week. Two sites where you can start researching these providers are www.eyalliance.org.uk/ and www.4children.org.uk/

Useful sites

As always, I do not necessarily know, like or trust any of these providers. This is just for your information.

https://www.childcare.co.uk/

http://www.greataupairs.co.uk/

www.eyalliance.org.uk/

www.4children.org.uk/

CHAPTER 27 —
Education

Introduction and purpose

Moving to another country involves more than just a successful relocation. For families, it's vitally important children are properly settled in the most suitable schools for their requirements. This chapter looks at the education system in the UK and discusses what options are available for schooling, as well as how to go about finding a school for your children, finishing with a quick look at universities.

Free education

Every child has the right to a free place at a state (taxpayer funded) school and a school may not refuse admittance to your child on the grounds of immigration status. If you select a state school for your child, it is usually your local council that decides the school your child attends.

Phases of schooling

A child in the UK would be expected to go through three phases of schooling:

- Pre-school or nursery (ages up to 5 years)
- Primary school (ages 5-11 years)
- Secondary school (ages 12-18 years)

School is compulsory for all children aged between 5 and 16 years. During the ages of 12 and 16 a child attends lower secondary school. At 16, they can either enter the workforce, enrol in vocational training or do what most do – continue studies until 18 at which point they can either enter the workforce or enrol at university.

The school year

There are three terms in a school year, interspersed with holidays. Following this is a long summer holiday. A typical school year looks something like this:

Time of Year	Session	Duration
September-October	First half of term 1	5~6 weeks
Late October	Half term holiday	1 week
October-December	Second half of term 1	5-6 weeks
Late December-early January	End of term holiday (Christmas)	2 weeks
January-February	First half of term 2	5~6 weeks
Mid February	Half term holiday	1 week

February-March	Second half of term 2	5-6 weeks
April	End of term holiday (spring)	2 weeks
April-May	First half of term 3	5~6 weeks
June	Half term holiday	1 week
June-July	Second half of term 3	5~6 weeks
Mid July-August	Summer holidays	6 weeks

The university schedule looks very similar except that the summer holiday runs beyond August, right through September. The new year begins in early October (although first year students usually start in September to give them time to get settled in). The other difference is that universities don't have half term holidays.

Grading in education

At school, grading in subjects runs from A (best) to F (weakest). F is considered a fail. At university, degree results are classified into one of the following:

- First class honours – overall score of 70% or higher (a distinction).

- Upper second class honours (or 2:1) – overall score between 60% and 69%.
- Lower second class honours (or 2:2) – overall score between 50% and 59%.
- Third class – overall score from 40% to 49% – still a pass.
- Below 40% – a fail.

School hours

Schools must be open for 190 days per school year. For most schools, the day starts between 8 AM and 9 AM and finishes between 3 PM and 4 PM.

The National Curriculum

A national curriculum has been devised by the Government and this is really just a roadmap giving key performance indicators and targets for a child to reach at various milestones of their education.

The National Curriculum is split into "Key Stages" 1, 2, 3 and 4, known as KS1, KS2, KS3 and KS4. Broadly, these key stages refer to the level of attainment a child is expected to reach by certain ages (or stages).

The National Curriculum is a way of standardising the education across all state schools. Very detailed information about the National Curriculum can be found by visiting https://www.gov.uk/national-curriculum

Pre-school

Pre-school starts at approximately three years of age. From the previous chapter, you might have noticed there are a number of options within the 3-5 year age bracket e.g. daycare, nursery, childminders and au-pairs. School before the age of 5 is not compulsory and in practice some children don't start until they're just about 6.

Three and four-year old children in England have a legal right to 15 hours of education a week, 38 weeks a year. In Northern Ireland, they get one year of taxpayer funded pre-school education.

Your employer might be able to assist with the cost of this education by issuing childcare vouchers. If not, you might be able to claim working tax credits. To be eligible, you and your partner both need to be working at least 16 hours a week.

Primary school

Primary school can be considered the foundation of secondary school. What's taught at primary school introduces students to subjects. Although the emphasis is on the core subject areas – literacy, mathematics and science, there will also be plenty of other subjects taught like history, geography, arts & crafts, music and physical education.

There is a standard optional exam at the end of Key Stage 2 in Year 6.

Secondary school

Secondary school is where the really serious learning begins. There are two types of schools – those funded by taxpayers (known as state schools) and those that are private (usually funded through fees charged directly to parents or guardians). In secondary school, subjects commenced in primary education are explored in much greater depth and there will be more pressure on students in terms of testing and exams. Plenty of homework and assignments will be set too. Some state schools are specialist schools – schools for extraordinarily gifted students. If your child has an aptitude for mathematics, music or something else, consider sending them to a specialist school.

Three years into secondary school, students will need to start specialising meaning they will drop subjects they're less interested in and focus on ones they like. They need to select subjects for their GCSE's (compulsory exams taken at the end of the fifth year or year 11 – when they're 16, or approaching 16).

Needless to say, English language and mathematics are compulsory.

The new National Diploma has a vocational bias to it – there is more emphasis on vocational training and work experience as opposed to raw academic prowess.

At 16, students can either go to work, attend vocational training or continue studying for 'A' levels (Advanced level). If they continue education with 'A' levels, they have to specialise even further, typically taking three (maybe four) subjects over two years. 'A' levels are the admission exams for university. In fact universities usually cite their entry prerequisites in terms of 'A' level results. For example, to get into Cambridge University, you need three 'A' levels, all at grade A.

Types of secondary school

State schools – most schools are state schools. This tends to be the default choice for most children. These schools of course follow the National Curriculum. "State schools" is more of an umbrella term. A state school can be a comprehensive school, a grammar school, a faith school or even a specialist school.

Comprehensive school – a type of state school where there are no academic criteria that need to be satisfied to enrol a child. These are also known as non-selective schools.

Grammar schools – these are selective state schools in that the children need to meet certain academic prerequisites to gain admission. In England and Wales, the test used to assess a child's academic ability is known as the 11-plus exam.

Faith schools – these follow the National Curriculum but as the name suggests, the emphasis is on a certain religion. They might have their own admissions criteria but still have to follow the National Curriculum. There is nothing stopping children from other creeds or even atheists from enrolling.

Private schools – sometimes also known as independent schools, these are schools which directly charge fees to parents/guardians and so they are not state-funded. They must still be registered with the Government and are inspected regularly. They also need not follow the National Curriculum. Some private schools might also have their own entrance exams aside from the 11-plus.

Confusingly, some independent or private schools are also known as public schools. To avoid any possible confusion, it's best to completely avoid the term "public school".

Independent vs. private schools

There is a subtle difference between private and independent schools. An independent school has a board of trustees or governors whereas a private school might simply be run by the owner, with no governing body.

Which is better – state school or private?

A private school is any school which is not funded using taxpayer revenue. They usually levy fees for tuition. There is an ongoing argument that private schools are better overall as they are presumed to have better and more up-to-date facilities, a better standard of teaching, better exam results and more extracurricular activities. But the reality is that there are state schools that can duplicate these advantages and moreover, there are great teachers in both systems. You could, for example, find a good grammar school to send your child.

Where will your child go to school?

Each school has what's known as a "catchment" area which delineates a geographical boundary around the school. These catchment areas are used for deciding which children will attend that school. It's usual for a child to attend a school if their residence falls within the catchment area for that school.

It is alternatively possible to send your child to another school even if you're living outside the relevant catchment area for that school. Your request must be granted if a vacancy for your child exists at this other school. If not, here are some other options:

- Find another state-funded school which does have a vacancy.
- Send your child to a school which charges private fees.
- Home schooling.

Each council has different procedures to follow when registering your child for a school. So you must first identify your local council. To do this, visit https://www.gov.uk/find-local-council and enter the post code of your home. You will then be given a link to the relevant council website. Within the subject of education alone, your council website will have a host of information on a range of topics. You will find information on term dates, registration for school and advice on day-to-day expenses such as clothing costs, meal costs, school transport etc. Assuming your child is enrolled at the nearest suitable school, transportation is free for children 5-8 years old provided they live at least 2 miles from the school, and it is free for 8-16 year olds if they live 3 miles or further from the school.

Universities

The UK unquestionably has some of the best universities in the world. There are a great many places to study and a seemingly endless choice of degree subjects. If you're looking for a university with more lenient admissions grades, consider a less popular one. Northern Irish universities, for example, because of their geographic location – being far away from Great Britain – might be worth looking at. In England, two top universities are Oxford and Cambridge (sometimes collectively known as "Oxbridge"). According to the World University Rankings published by Times Higher Education, they're both in the top 10 for 2021. Other good universities are UCL, Imperial College London, LSE and King's College London.

How much does a university education cost?

Undergraduate students who qualify for "home fee" status (meaning they're either British or EU students) will have their tuition fees capped by the Government. For the year 2020/21, this will be £9250.

According to Times Higher Education the average tuition cost for a medical degree can be as high as £58,600 pa for overseas students although the average annual tuition cost (across all subjects) is about £12,000. There are a number of finance options available including scholarships, bursaries and even loans from the Government. This is a matter well worth researching thoroughly, in order to explore all possible options.

Of course this is just tuition. There are also accommodation and living costs to think about. Times Higher Education also has detailed information on the various day-to-day living expenses students face.

Lessons learned

1) School is compulsory between ages 5 and 16. Many continue to do 'A' levels from 16 to 18, or else vocational training. After school, quite a few students enrol in university.
2) State schools are the norm and they're taxpayer funded. Your child would likely attend a school close to your home.
3) To find a school, you first need to identify your local authority (council) and then look for a link to education on their site.

4) Private schools potentially offer advantages over state schools, but they will charge you fees directly.

5) University tuition can be very dear, especially for overseas students. Consider a "less popular" university.

6) Thoroughly research available funding options for university study – bursaries, scholarships, loans etc.

Useful sites

https://www.gov.uk/help-school-clothing-costs

https://www.gov.uk/browse/childcare-parenting/schools-education

https://www.citizensadvice.org.uk/scotland/family/education/school-and-pre-school-education-s/help-with-school-costs-s/

CHAPTER 28 — *Bonus: English as a Foreign Language: The IELTS Test*

This is a bonus chapter. If you've not already done so, go ahead and pick up your bonus chapters from https://easyukmigration.com/bookbonus

You only have to do this once, and you will get all the bonuses for this book together in one email.

CHAPTER 29 — *Finding Work in the UK*

Introduction and purpose

The UK has one of the world's top economies (fifth largest) and has plenty to offer for those seeking a high standard of living. The work environment is diverse and tolerant so there's every chance you'll fit in well.

If you're in the market for a job in the UK, this chapter will give you some pointers on how to find one as well as the prerequisites. The Government has come up with a shortage occupation list. These are occupations for which candidates are deemed to be in short supply in the UK. If you're a healthcare professional, an engineer (any kind), a science teacher, a chef, an IT professional or an environmentalist, you will find it easier to get a job.

The job market

In the area of manufacturing, the UK might no longer be the "workshop of the world" but it does still lead in some areas in terms of research and development, particularly in aerospace and pharmaceuticals.

Service industries constitute a big chunk of the economy and are thus some of the largest employers in the country though appointments in this industry tend to be skewed towards the London area. Some other cities where large employers can be found in the financial sector are Newcastle, Norwich and Edinburgh.

How difficult it will be to find a job depends on the need there is for what you do. As outlined above, certain jobs are more highly regarded because of a shortage of candidates. Prior to 2020, the UK had an unemployment rate of under 5% however, the pandemic has taken its toll especially on jobs in certain sectors such as hospitality.

Employment-based visas and work permits

To legally work in the UK, you need both a work permit and an appropriate employment-based visa. But before you can even get your visa, you'll need a certificate of sponsorship which is something your sponsor (or employer) will arrange for you. Once you have this, you will be able to apply for your visa. Your employer will also arrange your work permit.

EU, EEA and Swiss expats are now treated the same as non-EU citizens (previously, you would not have needed a visa or permit to work).

If you want to spend longer than six months in the UK, then you will need to apply for a work visa (see Section 8 on immigration). Work visas are awarded on a points-based system. Points are awarded to you in your visa application on the basis of qualifications, language skills, earning potential and your existing funds.

A UK work permit is obtained by your new employer on your behalf and takes up to three months to be approved. It authorises you to do a specific job at a specific location. If you change employers, you'll need your new employer to get you a new work permit.

You will not be able to start working or even enter the country until you have your work visa. You can apply for your visa once you get your work permit. There is also a health surcharge to pay.

Note that there will also be a security clearance and this process will be longer if you're from one of these countries: Iraq, Libya, Russia, North Korea, mainland China.

Please refer to the chapter on visas for more information on work and business visas.

Where to search for jobs in the UK

There are many websites that advertise open positions. Among them, in no particular order, are Adecco, Jobsite, everyjobsite, Monster, Reed, Indeed, Michael Page, Blue Arrow, Adzuna, Careerbuilder, Totaljobs, and Trovit. Be aware that recruiters can advertise a given position in multiple places so there is likely to be overlap among these sites.

There are also a number of specialist sites that concentrate only on a particular industry or sector of the jobs market:

- Caterer – hospitality industry positions including pubs and bars.
- Charityjob – vacancies in charities
- Computer Weekly – IT positions
- CW Jobs – IT positions
- Design Week – vacancies around advertising, design, media, graphics etc.
- Exec Appointments
- Hays – management positions
- Just Engineers
- Madjobs – marketing, advertising and design vacancies
- Mandy – for positions in showbiz
- Music Jobs
- NHS Jobs – positions in the National Health Service (public healthcare) including managerial and administration.
- Prospects – for graduates
- Splashfind – top 100 job sites in the UK

It is said that half the jobs available at any time are not even advertised. Therefore, leverage your own list of contacts and ask around if anyone is hiring or knows someone who is hiring. LinkedIn is another good place to search. Ensure your LinkedIn profile is up to date.

There are companies which are always on the lookout for great talent. So if you spot a company that you really like the look of, another thing you could try is to send in a speculative application. It might help if you had some inside knowledge of the internals of this company as in its structure, the department you need to aim for and if possible, a contact name too.

Hints for preparing your CV

If you don't already have one, you will need to create a CV (résumé). If you do already have one, it's worth revising it. A UK style CV generally looks something like this:

Contact Details – appearing at the top should be your name, like a header in itself (do not put the words "Curriculum Vitae" at the top). Your professional title and contact details should be there too.

Employment History – most recent first. Give the company names, positions held, dates and responsibilities as well as achievements.

Education – most recent first.

Skills – these could be actual technical skills such as software proficiency as well as certifications and qualifications. Also, any "soft" skills, such as negotiation, leadership etc.

Interests – only if they're relevant to the job.

Referees – names and contact information of people who can give you an employment reference. Make sure you ask them for their permission first.

If there are any gaps in your employment history or education, be ready to explain them; for example, you were doing volunteer work, or you were on parental leave etc. On the other hand, if you were simply unemployed and seeking work, just be honest.

Very important: Do NOT include a photo on your CV. Also omit any personal information such as age, date of birth, gender and marital status. These can prejudice your application and for some of them, it's illegal for an employer to ask for them anyway.

As I said before, make sure your LinkedIn profile is up to date. The first thing a prospective employer is likely to check is your social media accounts. Be aware of this. If you use Facebook, it might be an idea to double check there's nothing on your timeline that's nsfw (not suitable for work).

Hints for preparing your covering letter

A good CV needs to be accompanied by a strong covering letter. The covering letter should complement your CV. Consider what the company's goals are in recruiting for this position and how you are part of the solution, in other words why you're a good fit. A good covering letter follows these general guidelines:

- It's short and to the point.
- Put the recipient's name and details at the top and specify the job you're applying for and job reference (if any).
- Make every effort to identify the person responsible for receiving applications and use their name in the salutation. So if this was Mr. Smith, then the salutation would be "Dear Mr. Smith,"
- If you don't know the name of the recipient, use "Dear Sir or Madam,"
- If you name a recipient in the salutation, the letter ends with "Yours sincerely," otherwise, it's "Yours faithfully,"

- In the body of the letter, explain why you're a good/the best candidate and how you would fulfil their requirements. Explicitly ask for the opportunity to attend an interview.

The importance of relevant keywords

Gone are the days of manually checking CVs (or so it would seem). With the sheer volume of responses that recruiters are now receiving, they have had to turn to artificial intelligence to help with the screening process. It's not unusual these days for a recruiter to use AI to screen your documents (CV and covering letter) for certain keywords or buzz words which are unique to that particular industry and profession. If your documents don't contain any of these keywords, your application will be filtered out without it ever being seen by a human being.

Unfortunately, I can't tell you what these keywords are because they're different for every industry and position being advertised. Sometimes these keywords will be embedded in the job advert itself. Your best bet is to ask a recruitment agent or do some other research.

All I'm saying is, if you don't get response(s) from your applications, this could be why – your documents don't contain any of the magic words they want to see.

Interviews

When you do get invited to an interview, here are some actions you can take to improve your chances.

- Take your CV and covering letter with you so you can refer to them in case there's something you're asked about and you need to quickly jog your memory.
- Research both the industry and company beforehand and prepare in advance questions to ask. They will probably give you an opportunity to ask questions at the end. Avoid asking about salary and benefits, especially at the first meeting.
- Always be early. Allow for delays along the way. You can always take a walk nearby while you're waiting (but don't get lost!) or just read a book.
- Dress appropriately. Research what they wear at that particular organisation. Or you could just be straightforward and ask beforehand (when you're invited to an interview) what the expected attire for the interview will be. Some people believe that even if the workplace is casual, you as a candidate should still be dressed in business attire. The golden rule is that it's always better being overdressed than underdressed.

- Use a firm handshake with good eye contact. Wait to be seated. Be polite to everyone, including (and especially) receptionists.
- Maintain appropriate eye contact during the interview itself.
- Listen carefully. Always wait for the interviewer(s) to finish their question, don't think you know what they're about to say. Don't interrupt.
- Answer the questions fully and politely and if you don't know something, say so.
- Avoid negativity. In particular, don't slag off your previous or current employer or workmates. If you do, your interviewer(s) might be inclined to think that they could get slagged off by you in the future.
- At the end, thank the interviewer(s) for their time and make sure you know what to expect next.

If you're unsuccessful, try to find out what you could have done differently or better, so you can improve for next time. It could just be that they had other stronger or more experienced candidates and that there was nothing wrong with you or anything in your background as such.

If you're successful, there could be more interview(s) such as with HR or other higher-ups. You might additionally be required to perform aptitude or other tests. Be prepared for these.

Salary expectations

Jobted has the latest figures for many occupations across the board. They cite an average UK salary in 2020 of £29,600 (US$38,500). At the top end of their spectrum, a dentist would be earning £72,000 (US$94,000), an engineer would be on £48,000 (US$62,500), and a pharmacist would get £40,250 (US$52,500). At the other end of the spectrum, a computer technician would be on £23,300 (US$30,300), a secretary would be on £22,000 (US$28,600) and a nanny would be earning £19,200 (US$25,000).

Also keep in mind the figures will vary across the country. As a rule of thumb, London has more opportunities and higher salaries, but it also has more candidates chasing those opportunities and a higher cost of living.

Healthcare insurance

When you get a new job, you might be accustomed to your employer automatically including healthcare insurance in your list of employment benefits. Some employers do this, but it is not universal. This is something you should check at the time of being offered employment and if private health cover is important to you, you should see if you can negotiate it with your employer.

Thanks to the National Health Service, private healthcare cover is not essential in the UK.

The professional environment

So what is a typical British workplace like? For the most part, people are polite and courteous. For meetings and appointments, punctuality is expected. Brits have a sophisticated sense of humour, often a dry sense of humour and the average workplace is often filled with wit. They are quite restrained in their opinions and will use hints when trying to give negative feedback. For example, if you devise a plan of work and somebody thinks it's no good at all, they might say "I think you should re-consider your plan" or "There may be better ways to do this".

You will be expected to dress professionally in most environments, unless of course your occupation requires some kind of special outfit or uniform. The financial sector is usually the strictest in terms of dress code. Attire for men usually means a business suit, though ties often seem to be optional. For ladies, it will be a lady's business suit or a dress. Some workplaces, especially very small companies, might have a much more relaxed dress code especially on Fridays (known as "dress-down day") but this is not universal so you should not take it for granted. You should check beforehand.

Lessons learned

1) You'll need a work permit, visa and sponsorship when working in the UK. Your employer will take care of all of these.
2) Invest time in preparing a quality CV and covering letter. Identify and make use of the correct keywords which attract a recruiter's attention to your application.
3) If your occupation is a specialist one, consider searching on a specialists' website.
4) Prepare well for the interview by researching the company and the industry. Think of some good appropriate questions to ask.
5) ARRIVE EARLY at the interview and be polite to everyone.

Useful information

Healthcare surcharge:

https://www.gov.uk/healthcare-immigration-application/pay895363/26062020_SPI_National_Statistics_T3_12_to_T3_15a_tax_year_2017_to_2018.pdf

Salary expectations in the UK:

https://uk.jobted.com/salary

CHAPTER 30 —
Your Employment Rights

Introduction and purpose

This chapter outlines your basic rights as an employee and where to go for further guidance.

Your employment rights

As an employee of a company or individual employer in the UK, you have a minimum set of basic rights, known as *statutory* rights. Among these rights are the following:

- You should be provided with a written statement about your job which clearly sets out basic details and the terms and conditions of your employment. In this statement, you can expect to find information about your job title, wage rate, anticipated hours of work, paid holiday and sick leave entitlements, details of any applicable pension scheme, minimum notice period, disciplinary process and procedure for reporting a grievance.
- You must be paid at least the National Minimum Wage. At the time of writing, this was £8.21 per hour if you're aged 25 and over but it will vary particularly if you're younger or if you are an apprentice. You must receive a payslip with any deductions shown. It need not be a hard copy.

- You must be given at least a month's notice of intention to dismiss you, unless you've been working for less than a month at the company.
- There are occupational health and safety laws which, among other things, mandate that you must be provided with a clean and safe working environment, there must be first aid equipment, washing facilities and drinking water. All equipment in the workplace must be safe for use. Where relevant, you must be provided with protective clothing.
- Under the same laws, you have a right to daily and weekly rest periods which means you must be given at least one day off in any 7-day period. You must be allowed to have an uninterrupted break of at least 20 minutes if you work for longer than 6 hours a day and it must be taken in the middle of the day (not at the start or end of the day). You're also allowed at least 11 hours between one working day and the next.
- You can't be made to work for more than 48 hours a week unless you consent and it's confirmed in writing.
- You have the right to paid holiday in every year. Full time employees get 5.6 weeks of paid leave per year and part-time staff will get a pro-rata amount of leave.

- Women can get 52 weeks of statutory parental leave in a year and men, 1-2 weeks.

Over and above your statutory rights, there may be other rights which are set out in your employment contract along with any terms and conditions. These are your *contractual* employment rights and they cannot restrict your statutory employment rights unless you consent to this. Even if you have no written contract of employment, your statutory rights still apply.

Your statutory rights likewise can't be limited if you're on a fixed term contract. A fixed term contract is for temps. It's a contract which expires on a set date in the future.

Under the Equality Act 2010, an employer is not allowed to discriminate against you if you're suffering from any form of physical or mental disability. Assuming you are suitably qualified for a job but you're disabled and your employer is made aware of this, they must make every reasonable effort to make adjustments in the workplace to ensure you are not disadvantaged as a result of your disability and that you have the same level of access to facilities in the workplace that everyone else enjoys. A couple of examples of this might include installing ramps for wheelchair users, or providing special orthopaedic chairs for staff with back problems.

The above gives you just the most significant and basic rights you have as an employee. For a more exhaustive explanation of your rights, you should go to the relevant Citizens Advice page at https://www.citizensadvice.org.uk/work/rights-at-work/

Useful sites

https://www.eoc.org.uk/employees-rights/

https://www.citizensadvice.org.uk/work/rights-at-work/

CHAPTER 31 —
Understanding Payroll Taxes

Introduction and purpose

I *was* tempted to start this chapter with that old cliché of there being only two things in life that are certain. But you already know it, so I'll spare you that.

In a previous chapter I described how to go about getting a job. In this chapter, I discuss how much money Her Majesty's Government will be taking from your earnings in the form of taxes, or rather, how much your employer will be forwarding to HM Revenue & Customs, which is the body responsible for collecting Government revenue, on your behalf.

Income taxes: The PAYE system

Previously, I touched on what people in certain occupations could expect to earn. But what would be the point of knowing gross salary expectations if you didn't also know how much of your pay you'd be entitled to keep?

Income taxes are progressive meaning the more you earn, the higher the percentage you pay. The good news is that the first £12,500 you earn in a fiscal year is tax free (though in practice, you might still have to pay National Insurance contributions – more on this below). This is known as your *Personal Allowance.* Your personal allowance will be higher if you can claim the *Marriage Allowance* or *Blind Person's Allowance,* but will be reduced if you gross over £100,000.

The lowest tax bracket (the "Basic Rate" of taxation) is 20p in the pound and this kicks in at £12,501. The next bracket is the "Higher Rate" of 40p in the pound and this kicks in at £50,001. Finally, there is a top rate of personal taxation, known as the "Additional Rate" of 45p which you won't reach until you're earning at least £150,001.

Every month (or every pay period), taxes are deducted from your pay in relation to what you earned in that period. This is the basis of the Pay As You Earn (PAYE) system. What you earned, the taxes you paid and any other deductions all get documented on your payslip which your employer will provide to you, though these days, it might be given to you in soft copy, not a paper copy.

In the example of Chapter 29 – *Finding Work in the UK,* for the fiscal year ending in 2021, our nanny had a gross income of £19,200. So her take home pay would be about £16,700, the pharmacist with a gross salary of £40,250 would keep just over £31,000 and the dentist who was grossing £72,000 would be getting about £50,000 take home pay. I got these numbers just by using the Government's own tax calculator.

If you're paid an annual salary, you will be paid monthly and your employer will deduct the taxes at source. If you're paid based on the hours you put in, you'll probably be paid weekly.

National Insurance contributions

The NI system was originally created to assist people who were sick and unemployed. Its scope was expanded in the 20th century to add funding for the National Health Service (NHS), the state pension and unemployment benefits.

You have to pay NI contributions if you're earning £183 or more per week or if you're self employed and earning a profit of at least £6475 per annum.

National Insurance number

You will need to get a NI number. This is compulsory if you want to work in the UK, whether you're British or not. Indeed, just opening any type of financial account like a bank account, or even a share trading account, you will be asked for this. For children growing up in the UK, their NI number gets allocated and sent out automatically as they're approaching the age of 16. For everyone else, it has to be explicitly requested.

To get one, you need to be present in the UK and you need to have the right to work. You then need to contact the relevant NI application hotline. Here are the details.

In Great Britain (England, Wales & Scotland):

Telephone: 0800 141 2075

Textphone: 0800 141 2438

Lines are open Monday-Friday,
08:00-18:00 (8 AM-6 PM)

In Northern Ireland:

Telephone: 0300 200 3500

Textphone: 0300 200 3519

Lines are open Monday-Friday,
08:00-20:00 (8 AM-8 PM)

A National Insurance number is a sensitive piece of information and should be kept confidential. It is rather like a SSN if you're an American or a TFN if you're Australian.

Not having a NI number should not delay your starting work, provided you've explained to your employer that your NI number application is pending, and you can prove to them you have the right to work in the UK.

Tax codes

Your tax code is a HMRC-devised code into which is built information like how much tax and NI contributions you should be paying as well as what allowance(s) you're entitled to. You'll find it on your payslip. It's crucial to make sure this code is correct. If it's not correct, you could be paying too much tax.

> ***Comment***: The interesting thing I've found with HMRC is that they don't give tax rebates in cases of over taxation. Instead, they simply use any over payment as a credit against any future tax liabilities.

It's particularly important to check you're on the right tax code when you change roles or employer. The tax code is usually a number followed by a letter, for example 1250L is a default tax code.

If your tax code ends in 'X', 'M1' or 'W1' you're being taxed according to an "emergency code". This will typically happen when your employer doesn't know the correct tax code to apply in your case – for example, when you've started a new job. It is very likely you'll pay more tax than you need to if you're on an emergency tax code but the good news is that emergency tax codes are temporary.

Tax relief

If you use your own money to purchase any items which are exclusively for business use or which you use in your employment, you can legitimately claim these as tax deductions. Examples of these would be uniforms for work, travel expenses incurred in meeting a client, or an orthopaedic chair used for work. If your employer happened to reimburse you, then of course you cannot claim that particular expense as tax relief. More details and an interactive tool to check if you can claim a particular expense can be found on the Government's tax relief page.

You must keep records and make the claim within 4 years of the end of the fiscal year in which the expense was incurred.

Tax returns

If you are simply a company employee, not self employed, and you have no other sources of income, you do not need to complete a tax return. But if you do have other streams of income, such as a side-business or you get rental income, you will need to fill in and lodge a tax return. This is known as a self assessment tax return.

Pensions

While not technically a tax, I've chosen this chapter to raise the subject of pensions simply because it counts as a payroll deduction and (I suspect) many younger members of the workforce see it as a form of taxation in that it's taken away before you even see it, and "retirement is such a long way off, it might as well be considered another tax!"

Pensions are a type of long term saving, the idea behind it being to fund your retirement, when you're no longer actively employed. There are broadly two types of pension in the UK – State Pensions, provided by the Government and private pensions.

State Pensions

The State Pension is funded through your National Insurance contributions. To be eligible for it, you need to have made at least 10 qualifying years of NI contributions or credits. To get the full amount, you need to have contributed 35 years of NI payments. If you haven't achieved this, your state pension will be paid on a pro-rata basis. If you have a Government Gateway account, you can check up on your contributions and qualifying years. If you've worked part-time or you have periods of unemployment, you might want to check what impact this has had on your qualifying years. In some cases, HMRC allows you to make top-up Class 3 NI contributions to compensate for any gaps in your record.

> ***Comment***: Dare I say it, the State Pension is woefully inadequate. At the time of writing, it was valued at a mere £134.25 per week (maximum). At this level of income, you're pretty much living on the breadline.

Private Pensions

Private pensions are usually organised and administered through your employer but the trustee and managers will often be another company. These are occupational pensions. When you start work with a new employer, you'll be auto-enrolled into one of these schemes. Your employer will usually warn you about this when you start work and you'll have the option to opt-out if you like.

Thus, if you go ahead with it, a percentage of your salary will be put into a pension fund and some employers will match this by throwing an equal amount of money into their employees' pension accounts. Then when you retire, the money accrued is used to purchase a pension.

You can also set up your own pension account, independent of what your employer is offering. These are known as Self-Invested Personal Pensions (SIPPs).

Note that there may be tax implications when you draw from a fund after you retire.

Lessons learned

1) Getting a NI number is essential if you're working for an employer and is a good idea even if you don't. This is one of the first things you need to do upon arriving in the UK.
2) Carefully check your tax code on your payslip, especially when you've just started at a new employer. It must be correct, or you'll pay too much tax.
3) Taxes are deducted at source by your employer. You will receive regular payslips which will give full details of what you were paid and the deductions.
4) You don't need to prepare a tax return unless you earn income from other sources or business. (It's usually okay to run your own business while you work for your employer though you should check this with your employer. Your own business shouldn't interfere with your employer's work, nor cause a conflict of interest).

Useful information

HMRC Personal Income Statistics, Fiscal Year 2017 to 2018:

https://assets.publishing.service.gov.uk/government/uploads/system/uploads/attachment_data/file/895363/26062020_SPI_National_Statistics_T3_12_to_T3_15a_tax_year_2017_to_2018.pdf

Individual tax calculator:

https://www.gov.uk/estimate-income-tax

Self assessment:

https://www.gov.uk/self-assessment-tax-returns

Tax relief:

https://www.gov.uk/tax-relief-for-employees

Apply for a National Insurance number:

https://www.gov.uk/apply-national-insurance-number

CHAPTER 32 — *Bonus: Self-Employment & Business*

This is a bonus chapter. If you've not already done so, go ahead and pick up your bonus chapters from https://easyukmigration.com/bookbonus

You only have to do this once, and you will get all the bonuses for this book together in one email.

SECTION EIGHT — IMMIGRATION

CHAPTER 33 — *Introduction to Visas*

Introduction and purpose

The UK left the EU in January 2020 and there was a transition period in effect which ended on 31 December, 2020. EU/EFTA citizens are now treated the same as anyone from any other country.

This chapter sheds light on what visa you need to enter and stay in the UK. The visa you need will depend entirely on your personal circumstances and your intentions (your purpose for entering the UK, how long you will stay and what you plan to do in the future).

There are all sorts of visas to fit different circumstances and to cover every detail of every visa is beyond the scope of this book. The best place to get this information (and be sure it's up-to-date) is from the Government visas web page.

Visas can be tricky. This book couldn't possibly hope to take the place of an immigration advisor. Therefore, if you're in any doubt about what to do, you should seek an immigration lawyer. This chapter provides a general overview of visas. The next chapter dives deeper into the Brexit changes.

Do you need a UK visa?

To help answer this question, a very good place to start is https://www.gov.uk/check-uk-visa.

Whether or not you need a visa is not guaranteed – as I said above, it depends on your circumstances.

Beginning January 2021, new visa rules apply. From 2021, if you're from the EU or the European Free Trade Area, you may enter the UK and stay for up to 6 months with no visa. Longer stays will require a visa. Citizens of a number of other countries such as Canada, the USA, Australia, Japan and many others are also potentially able to stay visa-free for up to 6 months. Use the link given above to check.

Citizens of British Overseas Territories and those from Commonwealth countries born before 1983 who qualify for the Right of Abode by virtue of a parent being born in the UK are able to live in the UK without a visa.

Visa tiers

You might occasionally come across the term "tier" as in Tier 1, Tier 2 etc. This refers to a category of visa.

- Tier 1 – investors
- Tier 2 – professionals
- Tier 3 – disused category
- Tier 4 – students
- Tier 5 – temporary workers

Types of visa

Study visa – if you are going to be in the UK for study at a recognised institution, this is the visa you will need. There are two types of student visa – a children's visa (for ages 4-17) and a student visa. You are allowed to work in the UK with either visa, although the child's visa is more restrictive. You will need to prove financial self-sufficiency in both cases. For both visas, there is a condition that you pay a health surcharge too.

Provided certain eligibility criteria are met, a general student visa also gives candidates the chance to apply for certain family members to come and join them in the UK.

Study English in the UK – this visa is for English language students studying on courses lasting from 6 to 11 months.

Standard Visitor visa – this is the visa you'd use for tourism, business (for example, attending a conference or business meeting), or if you're travelling to the UK for the purposes of medical treatment. It's considered a form of short-stay visa although it can be issued for as long as 10 years. You may not use it for work (paid or unpaid). More details can be found on the Standard Visitor visa Government page.

Transit visa – as the name suggests, this visa is used if you're transiting in the UK. It comes in two forms: (a) Direct Airside Transit Visa whereby you do not formally enter the country and you instead bypass border controls. In practice, you'll be confined to a restricted (transit lounge) area. (b) Visitor-in-transit visa whereby you *do* enter the country but you have only 48 hours in which to leave. If you need to stay longer, you will need to get a standard visitor visa.

A UK transit visa is not needed if you already have a standard visitor visa, marriage visa, EEA family permit or EU Settlement Scheme family permit.

Marriage Visitor visa – this visa can be used if you want to get married in the UK or register a civil partnership in the UK but it may not be used for staying permanently. Its term is for 6 months and may not be extended. On this visa, you may not access public funds nor bring in any other family members. You may not study or work (limited business activities are allowed).

Parent of a Child visa – this visa allows you to come to the UK if your child is attending an independent day school in the UK. The visa is issued for either 6 months or 12 months and is extendable repeatedly, until the child reaches the age of 12. You may not work or study on this visa, nor may you access public funds.

Family visa – if you're going to join a family member (child, spouse, partner, parent, sibling etc.), this is the visa you will apply for. The family visa might attract a health surcharge and you can extend or switch your visa to another one before your current visa expires. It takes from 8 to 12 weeks to reach a decision about your application.

You're not entitled to a family visa if your family member is temporarily in the UK on a student visa or work visa.

Visas for professionals

Permitted Paid Engagement visa – this would be used if you're coming to the UK to do a very specific one-off task of short duration. Examples of this would be to deliver a special lecture or take part in a fashion modelling assignment. You may not live in the UK for extended periods nor access public funds. As part of the eligibility requirements, you must have been invited to the UK by a UK-based organisation.

Skilled Worker visa – you must have a prior job offer with a salary of at least £25,600, have at least a school leaver's certificate, and speak English. This visa replaces the Tier 2 General Work visa which was scrapped from January 2021.

Health & Care visa – you need a job offer from the NHS or an organisation that provides services to the NHS. You may bring family members with you if they're eligible. On this visa, you're allowed to leave and re-enter the UK, and take up a second job, but no access to public funds is possible. One advantage of this visa is that because of the service you'll be doing for the country, no healthcare surcharge is payable.

Intra-company Transfer visa – this visa is applicable if your company back home has offered you a transfer to the UK while working in the same organisation. You'll have to pay the health surcharge. On this visa, you may not access public funds but you are allowed to leave and re-enter the UK, take a second job (up to 20 hours a week) and bring family members with you if they're eligible.

Minister of Religion visa – for this visa, you need to have been offered a position within a faith community. You are allowed to work for your sponsor, leave and re-enter the UK, do voluntary work and bring family members with you (if eligible). You may not access public funds, and a health surcharge is payable.

Sportsperson visa – the relevant sports governing body in your country must approve of your application and you need to be considered something of a world-class athlete or sports coach. You are allowed to work for your sponsor, play for your national team while in the UK, work as a sports broadcaster while in the UK, leave and re-enter the UK and bring family members with you (if eligible). You may not access public funds or start/ operate a business, and a health surcharge is payable.

Other visas

In no particular order, here are some other (mostly professional) visas.

- Temporary Worker – Creative and Sporting visa (T5)
- Temporary Worker – Government Authorised Exchange visa (T5)
- Temporary Worker – International Agreement visa (T5)
- Temporary Worker – Religious Worker visa (T5)
- Temporary Worker – Seasonal Worker visa (T5)
- Youth Mobility Scheme visa (T5)
- Innovator visa
- Start-up visa
- Global Talent visa
- Investor visa (T1)
- UK Ancestry visa

Prerequisites for work visas

The following list should be considered the minimum requirements:

- Valid passport or travel ID
- Proof of availability of funds to support you during your stay
- Proof of English language proficiency

In addition, all visas have eligibility requirements. You should follow the relevant link to see what the eligibility requirements are for your visa.

Application cost of your visa

To get an idea of what your application fee for a visa will be, use the visa cost estimator tool.

Lessons learned

1) The best place to start learning about visas is the Government's own visa page. This has clear and up-to-date information.
2) You may or may not need a visa depending on where you come from, why you're coming to the UK and for how long. To answer this definitively, use the Government's do-I-need-a-visa tool.
3) Visas changed in January 2021. More on that in the next chapter.

Useful sites

Main Government web page on visas and immigration:

https://www.gov.uk/browse/visas-immigration

Check whether you need a visa at all (do-I-need-a-visa tool):

https://www.gov.uk/check-uk-visa

UK Brexit transition – interactive tool to guide you on what actions to take:

https://www.gov.uk/transition-check/questions

UK Brexit transition – visa and immigration tool:

https://www.gov.uk/staying-uk-eu-citizen

Guidance for EU, EEA and Commonwealth subjects:

https://www.gov.uk/browse/visas-immigration/eu-eea-commonwealth

Confirm your settled/pre-settled status:

https://www.gov.uk/view-prove-immigration-status

Immigration Health Surcharge:

https://www.gov.uk/healthcare-immigration-application/pay

Visa application cost estimator:

https://www.gov.uk/visa-fees

CHAPTER 34 —
UK Immigration after Brexit

Introduction and purpose

As a result of Brexit, some changes were announced in 2020 which will affect EU nationals who are in the UK or who are travelling to the UK. This chapter discusses what happens from January 2021 and how Brexit might affect you going forward.

I am not an immigration lawyer. The information presented here is of a general nature. It cannot and does not take into account your specific needs and circumstances, and if you have any doubts about what action to take, you should seek your own independent legal advice. Everything given here was correct at the time of writing.

Use this visa and immigration tool to check the impact Brexit has had on you. If you're Irish or from outside the EU/EEA, Brexit has had no impact on you.

The Brexit transition

On 31 January, 2020, the UK left the EU and went through a transition phase which ended on 31 December, 2020.

In regards to deciding immediate actions for you/ your family to take, this will depend on your current circumstances. To help you begin, try this interactive tool on the UK Government website. It will take you through a few simple questions and at the end of them, you will get a personalised list of recommended actions for you to take which will also take into account your family and business (if any). This tool will work for you whether or not you're from the EU.

EU Settlement Scheme

If you're an EU citizen, provided you settled in the UK before 1 January, 2021, you'll be able to lodge an EU Settlement Scheme application. This is the scheme under which EU nationals can apply for either "pre-settled" status (also known as limited leave to remain) or settled status (also known as indefinite leave to remain). The deadline for lodging such an application is 30 June, 2021.

Settled status is available if you can prove you've lived in the UK for at least five years. The benefit of settled status is that you are then free from immigration control and don't need to make any further immigration applications, providing you don't leave the UK for more than five consecutive years (or four years if you're Swiss). Having settled status means you hold the same rights of living, working, healthcare and welfare as UK citizens.

If you have not yet spent five years in the UK, you might be able to obtain pre-settled status. You'll subsequently need to make an application under the EU Settlement Scheme for settled status, once you've lived in the UK for five years. Even with just pre-settled status, the important thing is that you'll still have the right to live, work and access healthcare in the UK.

You can check your immigration status online.

Brexit is complete. So what happens now?

If you're from **outside** Europe or if you're Irish, feel free to skip over this section and the next two sections: Brexit has no impact on you. Otherwise, if you're from the EU or the EEA, read on.

The Brexit transition period is now over. "Freedom of movement" ended on 31 December, 2020. In theory, EU citizens will no longer get preferential treatment. They will be treated the same as everyone else.

In January 2021, the immigration landscape changed. The Government's plan, inspired by Australia's points-based system, basically closed the borders to "unskilled" workers and those who can't speak English. Understandably, there is widespread concern about who will do jobs that Brits "don't want to do". Examples are aged care home workers, or construction site workers.

Full details about how Brexit affects you if you're from the EU/EEA can be found on the Government's page all about Visiting the UK as an EU, EEA or Swiss citizen which you should read. The following two sections below are just a summary.

Documents needed to enter the UK

From January 2021, EU, EEA and Swiss citizens may come to the UK for short trips with no visa. You just need a valid passport that remains valid for your entire trip. You will be able to continue using your national ID to enter the UK until 1 October, 2021. After then, you'll need to meet one of the following conditions:

- Have settled or pre-settled status under the EU Settlement Scheme
- Have an EU Settlement Scheme Family permit
- Have a frontier worker permit
- Be an S2 healthcare visitor
- Be a Swiss service provider

If you meet one of these conditions, you'll be allowed to continue using your national ID until at least 31 December, 2025.

As a rule, trips of longer than 6 months will require some kind of visa.

Business travel to the UK for Europeans

Travellers from the EU, EEA and Switzerland coming to the UK for a short business trip might not need a visa. Under the new points-based system, in most cases you're allowed to come with no visa for up to 6 months. You may engage in various business activities such as attending meetings, conferences, events etc. But you may not work as a company employee or be self-employed. You're also not allowed to directly sell goods or services to the public.

The process to follow before you travel to the UK on a business trip can be found here.

Visa application process

One piece of good news if you're from the EU, EEA or Switzerland, is that you won't need to attend an appointment at an overseas visa application centre to enrol your fingerprints. Your fingerprints won't be needed. Instead, you will use an app to enrol your photo. Thus you won't be impacted by the closure of visa application centres because of the pandemic. If you apply under the new Immigration Rules, you'll get a digital immigration status which can be securely accessed online. Non-EU nationals will continue to be issued biometric residence permits which are susceptible to delays in production, as well as theft and loss.

Skilled worker route

A new "Skilled Worker" route has replaced the Tier 2 General work visa route. The idea is to give preference to migration of skilled workers who speak English. In July 2020, the Government released more details of its points-based immigration system. In simple terms, to come in through the Skilled Worker route, you must:

- ✓ Have a job offer from an approved UK employer
- ✓ Meet a skill level of RQF3 or higher.
- ✓ Be offered a salary of £25,600 or the going rate for your occupation, whichever is the higher.
- ✓ Speak English.

Comment: These conditions are much less scary than they look. RQF3 is the equivalent of a British A-level (or HSC if you're coming from Australia.) So it's a school leaver's level. And a salary of £25,600 is well below the national average. As for English, well, most people speak it anyway. So the most challenging thing here is to get a job offer.

The great news for immigrants is that there is no annual quota on how many skilled workers may come in. Furthermore, there is also a concession on the salary condition. If your salary is lower than the amount specified above (but no lower than £20,480), you're still eligible to apply if you hold a relevant PhD, or your occupation is on the shortage occupation list.

Global Talent Scheme

A new Global Talent Scheme has opened up. This is an immigration path for top mathematicians, scientists and researchers, and no prior job offer is needed. Once again, there's no cap on the number of candidates coming through under this scheme. More details can be seen in a press release from January 2020. The Global Talent Scheme replaced the Tier 1 Exceptional Talent visa.

International students & graduates

Student visas are available provided you've been offered a place on a course, you know English (speaking, reading, writing, comprehension) and you can finance the course and support yourself. There is a new graduation immigration path for international students who graduate from Summer 2021 onwards. You'll be able to work or seek work at any skill level for up to two years (or three years if you're a PhD candidate).

Border control

If you're from any of the following countries and you have a biometric chip in your passport, you may still continue using the ePassport gates on arrival at UK immigration: Australia, New Zealand, Canada, USA, Japan, South Korea, Singapore. For the time being, anyone from the EU, EEA and Switzerland will also be able to use this entry method.

EU citizens and their EU family members who became resident in the UK before January 2021 may continue using their identity cards for travel at least until January 2026, provided their immigration status is covered under the EU Settlement Scheme. For the same group of people, ICAO-compliant identity cards will continue to be valid after 2026.

The use of "insecure" identity documents is set to be phased out for newly arriving migrants.

Low skilled immigration

With the exception of youth mobility and the seasonal agricultural scheme, there will not be any immigration path for lower-skilled workers. As outlined above, this is likely to cause great consternation to employers as they frantically try to fill positions Brits "don't want to do". According to the Government's own estimates,

70% of EU workers currently in the UK won't be eligible to apply under the skilled migration route.

Lessons learned

1) As of January 2021, the emphasis is now on skilled migration. The UK now has a points-based migration system. If you're coming to the UK on the basis of your talent and skills, you will be awarded points in your application based on various criteria such as education level and occupation. There is no annual limit on the number of candidates coming in through skilled migration.
2) If you're from the EU and you moved to the UK before 2021, you might be eligible to apply to stay in the UK under the EU Settlement Scheme.
3) The Government has launched a Global Talent Scheme for scientists, engineers and mathematicians, and you don't need a prior job offer from any UK employer. Again, there is no annual limit to the number of visas issued in this category.

Useful sites

Main Government web page on visas and immigration:

https://www.gov.uk/browse/visas-immigration

Guidance specifically for EU, EEA and Commonwealth subjects:

https://www.gov.uk/browse/visas-immigration/eu-eea-commonwealth

The Government's post-Brexit guide for Europeans:

https://www.gov.uk/guidance/visiting-the-uk-as-an-eu-eea-or-swiss-citizen

Check whether you need a visa at all:

https://www.gov.uk/check-uk-visa

UK Brexit transition – interactive tool to guide you on what actions to take:

https://www.gov.uk/transition-check/questions

UK Brexit transition – visa and immigration tool:

https://www.gov.uk/staying-uk-eu-citizen

Visiting the UK on business – Government advice:

https://www.gov.uk/visit-uk-business-trip

Confirm your settled/pre-settled status:

https://www.gov.uk/view-prove-immigration-status

Information on the points-based immigration system:

https://www.gov.uk/government/publications/uk-points-based-immigration-system-further-details-statement

Shortage occupation list:

https://www.gov.uk/guidance/immigration-rules/immigration-rules-appendix-k-shortage-occupation-list

The Global Talent Scheme:

https://www.gov.uk/global-talent

Press release about Global Talent Scheme:

https://www.gov.uk/government/news/boost-for-uk-science-with-unlimited-visa-offer-to-worlds-brightest-and-best

CHAPTER 35 —
The Life-in-the-UK Test

Introduction and purpose

Also known as the British Citizenship test, the Life-in-the-UK test is a test taken as part of the requirements to obtain Indefinite Leave to Remain. If you're unfamiliar with Indefinite Leave to Remain, I have a whole chapter on it.

The purpose of the Life-in-the-UK test is to assess your knowledge of British history, customs, values and knowledge of day-to-day life in the UK.

Who needs to take the test

Any person who wants to obtain Indefinite Leave to Remain. Note that this is not the only requirement for obtaining Indefinite Leave to Remain – just one of them.

Are there any exemptions?

You need only take this test if you're within the age range of 16-65. If you're outside this age range, you're off the hook. There is one other exemption and that is if you have a physical or mental condition which prevents you from taking the test.

Candidates with disabilities and impairments

If you are visually or aurally impaired, have dyslexia or some other condition likely to impact your performance on the test, you must make this known at the time of booking the test. This can be done by filling in a special arrangement booking form. This is also the form you would use if you were game enough to take the test in Welsh or Scottish Gaelic.

It takes a few working days to process your request and there is no guarantee they will accept it. Depending on your disability, you might be exempted from having to take the test at all.

What documentation is needed?

On arrival at the test centre, you will need to prove your ID and address. To do this, the following documents can be used.

For the photo ID requirement:

- Passport
- UK photocard driving licence
- EU identification card
- Biometric residence permit

- Approved travel document. Examples are UK certificate of identity, convention travel document or UK stateless persons travel document.

For the address requirement:

- UK photocard driving licence
- Bank statement
- Utility bill
- Correspondence from the Home Office with your name and address on it.

In the case of the latter three, the document must be an original (not a copy, and not printed from your online account) and it must have been issued no earlier than 3 months before your test date.

Administrative preliminaries

You need to book the test at least three days in advance and the cost is £50. In theory, the latest you're allowed to arrive at your test centre is 5 minutes before the test starts. Any later than this and your test could be cancelled on the spot, with no refund offered. Realistically, arriving 5 minutes beforehand does not give enough time for registration. You should instead aim to be there at least half an hour before the test is supposed to start. Bear in mind there will be other candidates for them to register too.

You must bring with you your government photo ID and proof of your address. These will be checked during registration.

This is your last chance to go for a comfort break or get a drink or whatever: Once you're shown your test workstation, you won't be allowed to leave until you've finished the test.

You will not be allowed to bring in any study materials with you. Any gadgets you have in your possession such as a tablet or smartphone must be placed into a locker allocated to you during registration.

Nobody will be allowed to accompany you into the test centre unless of course they too are actual test candidates. In any event, all candidates have their own partitioned workstations.

What is the test like?

The test is computer based and consists of 24 multiple choice questions selected randomly at the start, from a large database of them. This means if your friend is also taking the test in the same session as you, you likely won't get the same questions as each other. If you like, you can listen to the questions through headphones. You will be given 45 minutes to finish the test and there will be warning waypoints at the halfway mark, 10 minutes before the end and finally, a couple of minutes before the timer stops.

The test is of course delivered in English. The only exception to this is if you book a session at a Welsh test centre or a Scottish test centre. In that case, you will have the option of having the test in Welsh or Scottish Gaelic (if you wanted to). Otherwise, it can still be taken in English.

Before the test begins, you'll be given 4 warm-up questions just so you get the hang of how it works.

To pass the test, you must score at least 18 questions correctly.

How do you prepare for the test?

If you want a free resource, there are quite literally dozens of sites which are dedicated to this subject. All the sites I looked at offer both the study material as well as the ability to take mock tests. Just do a web search for Life in the UK or British Citizenship test and you'll uncover far more sites than you need. Many of these sites are quite generous in the amount of information they give for free. With some of them, you have the option to take out a paid membership and get some additional benefits but from what I can glean, these benefits often amount to the ability to track your test results over time and/or be able to study the material in languages other than English.

The Home Office have released an official study guide for the test. Another way to prepare for the test is to simply purchase a relevant book from Amazon.

Lessons learned

1) Subject to a few exceptions, everybody who wants to obtain British citizenship or Indefinite Leave to Remain must take and pass the Life-in-the-UK test.
2) This is a test of your knowledge of British customs, laws and history.
3) During the test, you will have 45 minutes to correctly answer at least 18 out of 24 questions.
4) There are many resources (free and paid) which you can use to study for this test. Among them are third-party websites, books on Amazon and the Home Office's own official guide (which is also available on Amazon).

Useful sites

Life in the UK Government site (to book a test):

https://www.gov.uk/life-in-the-uk-test

CHAPTER 36 — *Bonus: Indefinite Leave to Remain*

CHAPTER 37 — *Bonus: British Citizenship*

Chapters 36 & 37 are bonus chapters. If you've not already done so, go ahead and pick up your bonus chapters from https://easyukmigration.com/bookbonus

You only have to do this once, and you will get all the bonuses for this book together in one email.

SECTION NINE — RECREATION AND ENTERTAINMENT

CHAPTER 38 —

Bonus: Top Attractions in London

CHAPTER 39 —

Bonus: Top Attractions Outside London

CHAPTER 40 —
Bonus: Other Recreation

CHAPTER 41 —
Bonus: Cultural Events Around the UK

The chapters in Section Nine are all bonus chapters. If you've not already done so, go ahead and pick up your bonus chapters from https://easyukmigration.com/bookbonus You only have to do this once, and you will get all the bonuses for this book together in one email.

SECTION TEN — PREPARING FOR ARRIVAL AND SETTLING-IN

CHAPTER 42 —
Before Arrival: Your 50-Point Blueprint for a Successful Move to the UK

Introduction and purpose

This chapter is your essential blueprint for moving to the UK. It covers the weeks and months leading up to the big move and outlines what you need to do and when. Not everything will apply to you, so you'll need to decide what's relevant to you and skip over the rest.

How to motivate yourself

I know it's a ton of work to move anywhere especially overseas. There is so much to do. But the hardest part is usually the first step. So pick something really small and easy. It could just be a tiny book case or cabinet. Start going through it deciding what you'll ship and what you'll leave behind. Just trust me on this. Once you've done one thing, it motivates you to do the next task. You'll find your momentum builds with everything you do, and you will finish it all. Here is your 50-point blueprint for the preparation. Don't slavishly follow it – this is just a guide.

Countdown to moving day

6 months to go:

1) Start your housekeeping process now. Unwanted items should be either sold or donated, however there's more than enough time left to do this. At this stage, all that matters is to decide what will and won't be shipped and these decisions should be made before any removalist comes to inspect your home.

5 months to go:

2) If using a professional removalist, start researching removalist companies (*Chapter 8: How to Transport Your Possessions*) and then make bookings for inspections. The reason for starting this task so early is because they can get booked out many weeks into the future. Certain times of year could be very popular. So by doing this earlier, you potentially have a wider choice of shippers available to you.

4 months to go:

3) Start your job search (*Chapter 29: Finding Work in the UK*).

4) If the family pet is not going to the UK, start the search for your pet's new home. This process

could run for several weeks or even months before you find a satisfactory home. Start with friends, family and colleagues – ask around to see if anyone would be willing to accommodate your pet. You could also advertise.

5) Alternatively, if you've decided you're taking the family pet to the UK, start making enquiries and medical preparations with the vet. There are quite a few steps to this process and you need to make sure you do everything relevant for your pet, in the right order and at the right time. (*Chapter 9: How to Transport Your Pet(s)*).

3 months to go:

6) De-enrol from the electoral register – *doubly* important if you're Australian (see case study below). Does not apply if you're coming from a one-party state/dictatorship.

7) Advertise your car for sale if you're not shipping it. If you *are* shipping your car, be mindful of how much fuel you put in your tank between now and shipping day, keeping in mind that nearly all of it will need to be consumed before shipping day and any excess will have to be drained before the car is loaded into the container.

8) Start your visa research and then apply. It can take from 4 to 12 weeks to get approval. If you're going to the UK with a job already lined up, you won't have to do this because your employer should take care of your visa, work permit and certificate of sponsorship. **But you should verify all of this with them when accepting the job offer.**

2 months to go:

9) Consider setting up a UK bank account now (*Chapter 4: Money & Finance*). Don't worry if you're unable to do this from outside the UK – you can do it in your first week over there.

10) Investigate childcare options (*Chapter 26: Childcare in the UK*).

11) Start researching schools (*Chapter 27: Education*).

One month to go:

12) Collect your family's dental and medical records, letters of introduction and children's records.

13) If renting, advise your landlord/rental agency.

14) Book travel insurance for you and your family. This is to cover you en-route.

15) Arrange accommodation for your first two weeks in the UK (*Chapter 15: Renting*).

16) Touch base with your removalist to make sure everything is okay on their end. Check if you need to order in advance boxes & packaging, or whether they will bring the stuff on the day.

3 weeks to go:

17) Advise your friends, relatives, solicitor (lawyer), local council, insurance companies, accountant, hire purchase companies and stores where you have accounts, your gym, church and clubs, etc.

18) If your removalist is doing the packing, start consolidating and grouping together items in preparation for packing. If you're doing your own packing, start packing and labelling boxes now.

19) Order moth balls for clothing and silica gel sachets for furniture and electrical items being shipped (*Chapter 8: How to Transport Your Possessions*).

2 weeks to go:

20) If shipping your car, have it serviced. Ask them to pay particular attention to the battery as the car will be out of use for some time, while it's on the container.

21) Advise your bank(s) including credit card providers – do NOT close any accounts yet.

22) If transporting your washing machine or refrigerator, check with the instruction manuals whether these need bolting down for transportation. If you can't find your manual, replacements can be found online or else contact the manufacturers.

7 days to go:

23) Notify your post office to redirect any mail that comes to your residential address.

24) Alert federal and state taxation departments.

25) Do final clear out of garage and unwanted furniture.

26) Touch base with your removalist to make sure everything is still okay.

6 days to go:

27) Advise motor registry (licence & motor vehicle registration etc.). They might request you return the plates to them.

28) List essential items you will need on moving day.

5 days to go:

29) Contact your suppliers regarding disconnection of phone & final billing.

30) Organise final accounts for gas, water & electricity.

4 days to go:

31) Cancel regular arrangements e.g. gardening, cleaning etc.

32) Clean out medicine cabinet.

33) Empty garbage cans.

34) Empty steam iron, toaster, griller etc.

35) Drain fuel from lawnmower.

36) If shipping your car, drain the fuel until the tank is almost empty. Leave just 2 litres (half a US gallon) in the tank. You're allowed to put belongings in your car subject to the same rules/guidelines as the rest of the shipment – no weapons or other prohibited items, and no food, alcohol or tobacco.

37) Get rid of flammable materials (either discard or give to neighbours).

38) Launder and dry clothes. Also do any dry cleaning required.

39) Prepare any items requiring dismantling which are being moved e.g. modular furniture, trampolines etc.

1 day to go:

40) Tighten lid on all jars containing liquids.

41) Dismantle TV aerial if taking it.

42) Defrost and clean out interiors of fridge & freezer if taking them and give away any remaining food to family/friends/neighbours.

43) Touch base with your removalist one last time. This is worth doing and hopefully won't irritate them. Ask them what time they expect to arrive. Even an approximate time is better than no indication.

THE BIG DAY:

44) Consider packing a carton with essential things you will need when you first arrive e.g. bathroom effects, toilet paper & basic kitchenware.

45) Carry all valuables, cash and important papers with you.

46) Tighten taps (faucets).

47) Turn off water heater and drain it.

48) Check gas, electric switches and lights.

49) Check nothing has been left behind – don't allow the removalists to go until this is done.

50) Lock doors and windows and return house keys.

A FEW DON'TS:

- Don't pack perishable foods especially meat and dairy. The UK has strict biosecurity laws so it's best not to pack any food in your shipment.
- Don't pack alcohol or tobacco in your shipment.
- Don't pack weapons, ammunition, firearms or components thereof. None of these is allowed to be imported into the UK.
- Don't pack flammable liquids: kerosene, petrol, cleaning fluids, turpentine etc.
- Don't have your furniture French polished just before moving as it is very difficult to move without marking.
- Don't put fragile items or liquid in drawers, and don't overload drawers with too much linen or clothing.
- Don't put legal documents, money, jewellery or articles of extreme value in your shipment.
- Don't leave travel tickets, passports, cash or jewellery in any place where they could be packed.

CASE STUDY: Why early electoral de-enrolment is important

This information is primarily for Australians but is also of value to citizens coming from any other country where voting is mandated by law.

As you know, voting is compulsory in Australia and if you fail to vote in any election, you will be fined! Obviously, voting will be tricky when moving to another country and so the Australian Electoral Commission allows you to de-enrol. The process has improved since I did it. I had to download a form, print it out, fill it in by hand, and then scan and upload it to the site. It now appears that the paper step has been eliminated. You fill in a simple form online, authenticate it with a government-issued document number (passport or driving licence number) and then click submit.

When I moved from Australia, the AEC were suggesting doing this two months in advance of my moving date, which I did. Yet I still ended up with a fine because of delays in processing (turns out there was a local election just days after I left Australia). Thankfully, the form specifically requests what date you will be leaving Australia, and this is what saved me from having to pay that fine.

If you want to carry on voting at Australian elections while in the UK, you can certainly do so. You need to fill in the form which specifically allows you to do this, and you will then need to coordinate your voting with the Embassy of Australia in London. You can also subscribe to the AEC's mailing list to be alerted whenever there is a forthcoming federal election. The relevant forms are all at https://www.aec.gov.au/Enrolling_to_vote/overseas/index.htm

CHAPTER 43 —

After Arrival: Getting Oriented – Your 10-Step Quick Start Checklist

Introduction and purpose

This chapter discusses vital things you need to do in your first few days in the UK. Not everything will be applicable to you, so just skip what doesn't apply.

Recovering from the journey

So you've just arrived in the UK and you've just passed immigration. I get it, you're tired and you don't feel like doing anything. If so, that's fine. Take the rest of the day off. Go for a walk and stretch your legs. This is even more important if you've crossed several time zones as it helps you adjust to the local time zone more quickly by forcing you to stay awake until bed time. Equally important is to keep up your fluid intake for at least 24-48 hours. Avoid tea, coffee and coke (soda) which will dehydrate you.

It's vitally important to have already set up a place to stay for your first few days even if it's only a hotel or bed & breakfast place. This chapter assumes you've done that. Following is your essential checklist for what to do in your first two weeks.

Your first week in the UK

Once your energy levels have recovered, the following is a list of things you can start working on – except the first two, which you might even want to do the day you arrive. The other actions can wait until you've caught your breath. Some of these things take time to sort out, so it's best to get the ball rolling at your earliest convenience.

Step 1. Pick up a SIM card – you can do this at any shop, even the ones in the airport. And don't worry about which provider you've chosen, this can easily be subsequently changed by getting a new SIM card and then transferring your number over to the new provider.

Step 2. Pick up an Oyster travel card – this is for travelling on London transport. It might even make sense for you to do this while travelling from the airport to your accommodation. This will be especially useful if you're going to be based in/around London. The other thing to consider is a Railcard if you're aged 16-25. This will give a one third discount for off-peak fares.

Step 3. Apply for a National Insurance number (Chapter 31 – *Understanding Payroll Taxes*). This is still recommended even if you're not going to work for an employer.

Step 4. Open a UK bank account (Chapter 4 – *Money & Finance*). You might initially try an online bank which does not require proof of address.

Step 5. Enrol with the National Health Service (NHS) by finding a GP and registering yourself and your family (Section 3 – *Your Health*).

Step 6. Identify and locate your local hospital (Chapter 12 – *Hospitals and the EHIC*). It's better to do this before you really need to.

Step 7. Find a dentist and register (Chapter 11 – *Finding a Dentist in the UK*).

Step 8. If applicable, find schools for your children (see the section "Where will your child go to school" in Chapter 27 – *Education*).

Step 9. If applicable, arrange childcare (Chapter 26 – *Childcare in the UK*).

Step 10a. If applicable, start searching for work (Chapter 29 – *Finding Work in the UK*).

Step 10b. Alternatively, if you've decided to operate a business, do any necessary research and then set up your company (Chapter 32 – *Self-Employment & Business*).

Your second week in the UK

Hopefully you've had a chance to settle in, find your bearings and action all of the above that's applicable. Don't worry if you've not been able to finish some of the items above. It's still early days. However at this point, you might choose to review your accommodation arrangements. Are they still suitable and convenient for you? Should you find something a bit more permanent? (Section 5 – *Finding Your Accommodation*).

Once you've got all of the above under control, it's not too early to start thinking about recreation. Think clubs, gyms and so on (Section 9 – *Recreation and Entertainment*). You could start by exploring your local area on foot.

CHAPTER 44 —
A Few Final Words

Why you should move to the UK

Well, this is it. You've reached the end of the book. Hopefully this book has been of some benefit to you.

The UK has so much to offer. Its proximity to Continental Europe makes it a convenient base for those who have to or want to travel. You're only hours away from Europe and the Mediterranean, and just 7½ hours from New York. Plus there is so much choice in everything – availability of things to buy, choice of places to live, choice in education and choice of occupation. And with today's trend of working remotely, many people are no longer tied to any particular geographic location because of work. We have a public health system which although is not perfect, is in most cases adequate and you can be treated without fear of being bankrupted.

Far and away the UK's best advantage (in my opinion) is the sheer freedom. Freedom from interference from anyone or anything, and the right to live your life the way you want. If you disagree with something, you're allowed to speak up. We are a proud democracy with proper rule of law. It's okay to criticise the government or politicians without fear of being interrogated, imprisoned or worse. Everyone has rights in the UK, whether they're guilty of a crime or not. These are freedoms that everyone ought to treasure because they're not available worldwide. The UK is a haven for anyone seeking political asylum.

I know that moving is a big deal but when your move is complete and you're settled in, you will not regret moving to the UK.

I wish you a very pleasant stay.

How can I help you?

Is there anything else you'd like to know? How can I help you with your move and transition to the UK?

And what did you think of this book? Did it meet your expectations? Was there anything you expected to see in this book that was not covered? I intend to release updates to the book over time so your feedback would be invaluable. Please visit https://easyukmigration.com/feedback and fill in the simple form to let me know your thoughts. I also look forward to hearing about your success story in moving and how this book helped you.

And if you purchased this book through Amazon, would you please now go ahead and leave a 5-star review for it. Many thanks in advance.

This is the beginning of your journey to the UK. Happy moving!

Made in the USA
Coppell, TX
08 August 2022

81137580R00174